BFI Film Classics

The BFI Film Classics series introduces, interprets and celebrates landmarks of world cinema. Each volume offers an argument for the film's 'classic' status, together with discussion of its production and reception history, its place within a genre or national cinema, an account of its technical and aesthetic importance, and in many cases, the author's personal response to the film.

For a full list of titles in the series, please visit
https://www.bloomsbury.com/uk/series/bfi-film-classics/

W0234884

For my mother, Carolyn Lamm

Riddles of the Sphinx

Kimberly Lamm

THE BRITISH FILM INSTITUTE
Bloomsbury Publishing Plc
50 Bedford Square, London, WC1B 3DP, UK
1385 Broadway, New York, NY 10018, USA
29 Earlsfort Terrace, Dublin 2, Ireland

BLOOMSBURY is a trademark of Bloomsbury Publishing Plc

First published in Great Britain 2025 by Bloomsbury on behalf of the
British Film Institute
21 Stephen Street, London W1T 1LN
www.bfi.org.uk

The BFI is a cultural charity, a National Lottery distributor, and the UK's lead organisation for film
and the moving image. We believe society needs stories. Film, television and the moving image
bring them to life, helping us to connect and understand each other better. We share the stories
of yesterday, search for the stories of today, and shape the stories of tomorrow.

Cover artwork: © Sam Richwood
Series cover design: Louise Dugdale
Series text design: Ketchup/SE14
Images from *Riddles of the Sphinx* (Laura Mulvey and Peter Wollen, 1977), © British Film Institute;
Penthesilea: Queen of the Amazons (Laura Mulvey and Peter Wollen, 1974), Laura Mulvey–Peter Wollen
Film stills courtesy BFI National Archive

A catalogue record for this book is available from the British Library.

Library of Congress Control Number: 2024949484

ISBN: PB: 978-1-8390-2685-0
        ePDF: 978-1-8390-2687-4
        ePUB: 978-1-8390-2686-7

Produced for Bloomsbury Publishing Plc by Sophie Contento
Printed and bound in India

To find out more about our authors and books visit www.bloomsbury.com
and sign up for our newsletters.

Contents

Acknowledgments

Laura Mulvey's generosity made this book possible. We had many conversations about *Riddles of the Sphinx* in which she answered my questions and deepened my interpretations. I wish I could have spoken with Peter Wollen (1938–2019), but in the course of writing this book, the feeling that I was lucky to encounter the brilliant, hopeful worlds he created in collaboration with Laura kept growing until gratitude and awe replaced the feeling of loss. Conversations with Larry Sider, full of his enthusiasm, expertise and kindness, gave the project a real boost. Sincere thanks to Anna Coatman, Rebecca Barden and Sophie Contento for their helpful suggestions and patience. Jade Evans navigated the Peter Wollen collection at the BFI National Archive on my behalf with real skill. Megan Swihart Jewell, Melanie Noel, Anna Backman Rogers and Nathan Shields gave crucial support along the way. As I wrote about the voices in *Riddles*, I thought a lot about my father, Donald Lamm (1942–2021), and his work at the telephone company. I am very sad I didn't reach him in time. His death will always haunt my writing. Most of all, I want to thank Michael Eng for his sharp intelligence and abundant love for me and Lady.

Introduction: A New Language of Desire

'Not just a cinematic text but a major piece of feminist poetry' – this is how feminist art historian Griselda Pollock described *Riddles of the Sphinx* (1977) in 2010.[1] Written and directed by Laura Mulvey and Peter Wollen, *Riddles* is a classic of the feminist avant-garde cinema that emerged in the 1970s to expand the images and sounds through which women recognise themselves. A full-length 16mm colour film produced with financial and institutional support from the BFI, this 'piece of feminist poetry' draws from a psychoanalytic understanding of the mind and invites viewers to see feminism as more than a political project for women's equality. In *Riddles*, feminism is a poetic practice that works-through the mythical images narrowly defining 'woman' and allows those images to slip from their moorings and float, suspended in a cinematic world akin to a dream, full of wishes and uncertainties.

Riddles deploys an array of tools from avant-garde cinema – Mulvey calls them 'tropes' – to disrupt expectations of how films should look and sound.[2] Language is one of these tools, as the film incorporates a heterogenous set of written forms – citations, poems, monologues, intertitles, theoretical essays and diary entries. This set of texts shows us that film is a 'language' composed of shots, forms and devices that often reinscribe long-standing myths of 'woman' and occlude differences among women. Devoted to the possibility that avant-garde cinema can undo these myths, Mulvey and Wollen place their texts in unpredictable relationships with their images as well as the slightly eerie sounds of a hypnotic score that winds through the film and evokes feelings that hover at the edge of consciousness. This defamiliarising aesthetic opens spaces in the imagination where the complexity of women's relationships to images can become visible, their voices can become audible and both can be perceived as valuable.

Riddles was shot on location in London in the late summer and autumn of 1976 and reflects the flourishing of independent and experimental film in Britain, the emergence of feminist art, film and theory and the rise of decolonial cinemas around the globe. The film illustrates Wollen's concept of 'counter-cinema' from his 1972 essay on Jean-Luc Godard, as it challenges the orthodox codes of film-making and interrupts the dominance of glossy cinematic images produced by Hollywood for easy consumption.[3] Like so many leftist film-makers of their generation, Mulvey and Wollen were inspired by the revolutionary, anti-establishment spirit of the times and created cinematic alternatives to Hollywood with the hopes of intervening in the dominant cultural order. The Women's Liberation Movement, which had been gaining momentum in Europe and the US since the mid-1960s, is part of this resistance, and *Riddles* reflects the movement's focus on making images sites of collective political struggle. Activist intellectuals led by their cinephilia into writing about films and then making them, Mulvey and Wollen saw that Hollywood had been solidifying icons of 'man' and 'woman' that make the subordination of women seem natural and reduce their images and voices to mirrors for reflecting the desires of others.

Coming of age in the 1960s and early 1970s, Mulvey and Wollen's collaboration attests to the extraordinary convergence of transformations – political, intellectual and aesthetic – that took place during this historical period. Their approach to film-making can also be traced to the upheaval of World War II. Mulvey was born in 1941 and Wollen in 1938. They both reflected in writing on their childhoods in wartime Britain. Mulvey recalls that for the first six years of her life in the Sussex countryside, she did not see any moving images, which made the films she saw in London after the war vivid fragments dense with emotional resonance. Images from Robert J. Flaherty's *Nanook of the North* (1922), Michael Powell and Emeric Pressburger's *The Red Shoes* (1948), Jean Renoir's *The River* (1951) and Luis Buñuel's *Robinson Crusoe* (1954) are inscribed into her memory. They are the source of what she would later identify as 'afterimages'.[4] In 'An Alphabet of Cinema', Wollen connects his memories of the Blitz – hiding in closets and under tables in his home in the North of England, 'listening to the buzz of rocket bombs overhead' – to the 1942 Disney film *Bambi*, the first film he ever saw.[5] For Wollen, *Bambi* is 'a war film' and the 'source of his cinephilia'.[6] Together, their writings portray film as a repository that holds the unpredictable entanglements of history and personal memory.

Mulvey and Wollen attended the University of Oxford in the late 1950s and early 1960s. She studied history at St Hilda's College and he read English Literature at Christ Church. They met in the spring of 1963 through the social world of Oxford students. As a teenager, Mulvey became enamoured with French cinema, and it wasn't until she graduated from university that she 'fell in love' with Hollywood cinema.[7] Never faithful to aesthetic hierarchies, they were both 'electrif[ied]' by the serious attention paid to American Westerns, melodramas and gangster films in the pages of the French film magazine *Cahiers du cinéma*.[8] Pursuing their cinephilia together, Mulvey and Wollen spent their Sundays travelling across London to 'catch' Hollywood double bills.[9] In Britain, this was a subversive love. Although Hollywood produced a fine-tuned and glossy product, it also defied the elitism of British culture. Hollywood gave their generation of 'left-wing cinephiles' an arena for Oedipal rebellion.[10]

The Women's Liberation Movement punctured this romance. As Mulvey reflects in 2015, the feminism that took hold in the 1970s 'shocked [her] into seeing with new eyes the movies that [she] had loved so unquestionably'.[11] Mulvey explains that '[p]reviously, [she] had quite happily, and probably unconsciously, watched Hollywood films with an assumed masculinity in keeping with the films' cinematic style and language.'[12] Like experimental film, the Women's Liberation Movement challenged her habitual ways of seeing, and by revisiting this shift, she draws on what would become the focus of her film-making, writing and activism – a feminism engaged with psychoanalysis to investigate how viewers identify with cinematic images and absorb their political meanings. Mulvey and Wollen did not abandon Hollywood cinema, but feminism, combined with the innovations of radical film, gave them new ways of experiencing it.

To resist unconscious absorption in the flow of cinematic images, *Riddles* was composed as a book that places the spectator in the position of a reader. The film begins with a static close-up shot of *Midi-Minuit Fantastique*, a French film magazine published from 1962 to 1972, which Mulvey and Wollen found at a film bookshop in Paris.[13] Held by two anonymous hands – actually, they are Mulvey's – the magazine is placed diagonally across the screen as though viewers are looking over a reader's shoulder. Located out of the frame, Mulvey's act of reading invites viewers into the scene and creates a space for their imaginative associations. The edition of the magazine presented, titled 'Vamps Fantastiques', is from July/August 1962. A 'vamp' is a femme fatale or a predatory woman, and the magazine submerges viewers in the realm of erotically charged myths and fantasies. The cover features an image of Mary Morris as the Hindu goddess Kali in *The Thief of Bagdad* (1940), a Technicolor film produced in Britain and based on *One Thousand and One Nights*. Although viewers get only a glimpse of the faded black-and-white cover, the still of Morris in costume evokes the bejewelled opulence of an orientalist fantasy in 'brownface' and attests to imperialism's

collapse of the foreign, the feminine and the decorative. With large sans serif letters of a cool, bright turquoise blue, the title appears over the essay 'Le Mythe de la Femme' by the Belgian Surrealist Félix Labisse. Mulvey flips through the pages at a leisurely pace, her hands bringing touch to the scene of reading. The black letters printed on the yellowed pages create a blur that 'murmurs'.

As she turns the pages of *Midi-Minuit Fantastique*, an epigraph from the work of the modernist writer Gertrude Stein appears. Framed by a turquoise-blue rectangle, the poetry of Stein's line, with its playful, syntax-defying meditation on wishing, hints at

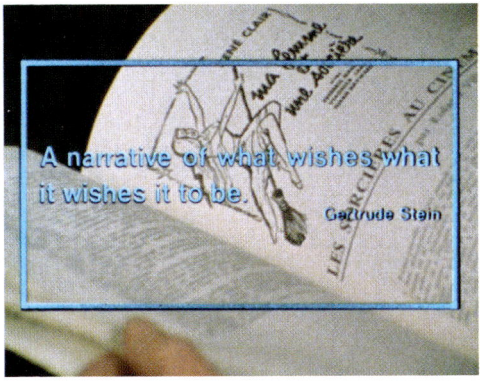

the experimental writing Wollen incorporated into the script and connects it to the hopes expressed by the arrangement of a story. With these images of writing, Mulvey and Wollen break the spell of verisimilitude and interrupt the fiction that we can *see through* images of women and the truths to which they presumably give us access.

The table of contents for this cinematic book appears on screen and announces the film's seven chapters. Quoting the distinct sequences of Godard's *Vivre sa vie* (1962) and Chantal Akerman's *Je tu il elle* (1974), the placement of the chapters at the centre of the frame foregrounds the construction of the cinematic narrative and its interruption.[14] With their typographic boldness and Technicolor blue, the letters layered over the magazine fracture the image and announce the leitmotif of colour to deepen its sensuous effects. The letters tell us Mulvey and Wollen approached cinema as a form of writing that can inscribe words and images on top of those from the past and reveal the voices, histories and sensations they hold. In this cinematic palimpsest, the passive viewing normally fostered by film has become an active scene of reading, and the normally smooth surfaces of images become labyrinthian.

As the film continues to display pages from *Midi-Minuit Fantastique*, viewers see that they are decorated with illustrations,

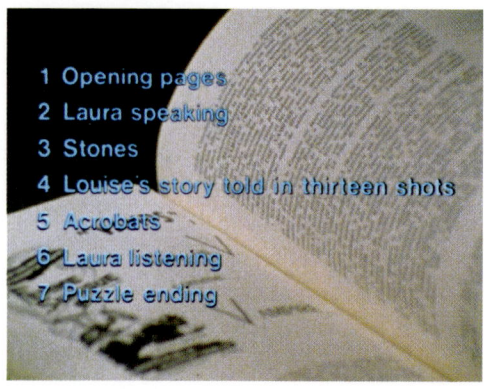

film stills and movie posters from cult and B-film genres such as horror, science fiction and fantasy. There are mythical images of women as witches, harpies, hybrids of women and birds, spider ladies, seductive and strange beasts with tattooed skin, mermaids with flowing hair and seductively curved fins. Symbolically dense and full of sensuous energy, the images of women in 'Vamps Fantastiques' materialise what Mulvey and Wollen call 'male fears and fantasies', a refrain that appears throughout their work. They also reflect their interest in cinema's origins in visual attractions such as the circus, magic shows, amusement parks, nickelodeons and peepshows.

A photograph of Greta Garbo as the 'Sphinx Moderne' is one of the woman/animal hybrids. Garbo's pale white face and her sly, sidelong glance has been superimposed over an image of this giant limestone monument in the Egyptian desert, and the waves of her bob echo the eroded ridges of the Sphinx's giant torso. Interrupting the flow of flipped pages, the still image introduces Egypt as the film's mythical past, and through its association with imperial archaeology, the idea of excavation. A fraught symbolic geography where ideas about the 'civilisation' attributed to Europe and the 'primitive' attributed to Africa have been fought over to justify racial hierarchies, Egypt points to the directors' implicit attention to the racism cinema borrows from western imperialism.

Notoriously elusive, Garbo was a movie star who transitioned from silent film to the talkies. Her image evokes that history, reminding us that the cinema was, as Mulvey writes, 'born mute'.[15] So it makes sense that this reading of 'Vamps Fantastiques' takes place in silence and defies the expectation to hear a score that will map the emotional landscape of *Riddles*. In addition to cinema before the 'talkies' and its heavy reliance on texts, this silence may allude to independent film's turn away from synchronised sound in the 1960s to signal its distinction from commercial cinema.[16] And because music often encourages the illusions and identifications of cinematic narratives, the silence could be interpreted as a feminist refusal. It clears an acoustic space for listening to the voices in the scenes that follow.

The chapters of *Riddles* are not arranged to tell a linear story. They are closer to stanzas in a poem than a sequence of events. The first chapter, 'Opening pages', is underway when the table of contents appears and shifts the emphasis from looking to reading. 'Laura speaking', the second chapter, portrays Mulvey sitting at a desk and addressing the audience as the writer and director of the film. She introduces the voice of the Sphinx and links her to the film's feminist themes. Following 'Laura speaking' is 'Stones', a seven-minute chapter comprising found footage of the Egyptian pyramids and the Great Sphinx of Giza. Focusing on the Sphinx's closed lips, 'Stones' features the film's electronic score and its intimate dialogue with its images.

At the centre of *Riddles* is 'Louise's story told in thirteen shots'. The fourth and longest chapter, 'Louise's story' demonstrates Mulvey and Wollen's interest in bringing the poetics of cinema and narrative content together. On one level, the story of this chapter is very simple: Louise (Dinah Stabb) is a young, white, middle-class woman living in London in the 1970s. Absorbed in the pleasures of raising her infant daughter Anna (Rhiannon Tise), Louise begins a process of discovering what being a woman and a mother means to her. And yet, because historically the value of women has been determined by the images they project, and because, so often, those images keep them fixed in place, this story is quite complex. To render its intricacy, Mulvey and Wollen have composed a circular and layered portrait of Louise that strains at the edge of recognition.

Key to this complexity are the 360-degree pans, the 'shots' composing the chapter. Borrowed from Sergei Eisenstein and Godard, they highlight the connections between the film's formal innovations and its feminist themes.[17] Circling like a film reel or an LP record on a turntable, the pans range from two to ten minutes in length. They track Louise as she moves from the domestic spaces of her home to the public world of work. This formal innovation made an impression. When *Riddles* premiered at New York City's Film Forum in March 1978, J. Hoberman wrote a review of the film in the *Village Voice*, aptly titled 'Our Mother, the Sphinx'. He noted that the pans 'rotate the boundaries of [Louise's] world in a kind of slow delirium'.[18] Through these altered emotional states, *Riddles* sculpts Louise's everyday life into a series of tableaux and places it at the centre of avant-garde cinema. The Sphinx (Mary Maddox), whose voice we first hear in 'Louise's story', guides this journey.

With their slow kaleidoscopic movement in which colours, textures and sounds come together and pull apart, the pans signal the turns of feminist revolution. Watching Louise appear in fragments, viewers see her oblique response to the Women's Liberation Movement and its impact on Britain in the 1970s. An interracial and potentially queer friendship with Maxine (Merdelle Jordine), a Black woman, arises out of Louise's attachment to her daughter and offers a glimpse of the desire to make racial justice part of feminism's vision of transformation. Following Louise as she shifts her place in a culture that revolves around white patriarchal masculinity, *Riddles* opens spaces in which we can see women writing what Mulvey identifies in her well-known essay 'Visual Pleasure and Narrative Cinema' (1975) as a 'new language of desire'.[19]

Riddles has a symmetrical structure. The three chapters that follow from 'Louise's story' are counterpoints to the first three.

The fifth chapter, 'Acrobats', portrays women as gymnasts and circus performers. Printed in fluorescent colours, the playful range of their movements contrasts with the static muteness of the Sphinx's mouth in 'Stones' and evokes the physical energy and freedom unleashed by Women's Liberation. 'Laura listening' announces the symmetrical structure of the chapters most explicitly. By portraying Mulvey listening to and transcribing a recording of her address in 'Laura speaking', 'Laura listening' creates an image of a woman in a self-reflective relationship to her own voice. The seventh and final chapter, 'Puzzle ending', depicts a mercury puzzle made of blue plastic. Like the scene of reading in 'Opening pages', the person playing the game is Mulvey, and again, her gaze is outside the frame. Her silent play with this visual riddle invites viewers to see the puzzles of patriarchal thinking women have to navigate.

Patterns of sound and silence bring viewers into the intricacy of these chapters. Larry Sider, one of the film's sound editors, explains that sound is usually considered separate from a film's images. It is a decorative afterthought 'waiting patiently in the background' as the score often is during film production.[20] Evoking the secondary status of women and the humility expected of them, Sider's descriptions reveal the gender hierarchies that infiltrate sound and shape what we hear and how we listen. At the same time, he makes the case that music 'imbues the image with emotional or cultural resonance' and 'guide[s]' the attention of viewers, sculpting how they see.[21] In Riddles, Mulvey and Wollen worked with sound to lead viewers away from dominant images of women.

In this book, I follow how the sounds of Riddles invite us to become listeners of the voices Women's Liberation brought into audibility in the 1970s. As So Mayer argues, Riddles is an example of a 'radical auditory cinema' that emerged in the 1970s and 'audition[s] a new kind of audience able to listen to women'.[22] By loosely intertwining images, text and sound, Mulvey and Wollen created feminist modes of listening attuned to women's desires and fantasies. These shared ways of attending to the meanings of images and words that spill beyond denotation draw from the responsive listening of psychoanalysis. Often called the 'talking cure', many forget that an analyst attentively listening is the centre of psychoanalysis. The psychoanalytic listening of this film attunes viewers to the emergence of women's voices as they challenged the standard language for representing women.

In *Riddles*, the voice, intimately linked to subjectivity and its unpredictable weave of language, body and history, is an object of feminist desire. To reveal how Mulvey and Wollen composed their film to pursue this desire, I read it as an essay film, a genre that shuttles between film and literature to create a poetics of interpretation that breaks open ossified perceptions. Linking the features of the essay film to Mulvey's and Wollen's own writing, I follow how *Riddles* takes viewers through an experience akin to what Sigmund Freud identified in 1914 as 'working-through'.[23] Though American feminists declared Freud the enemy in the 1970s, in Britain, feminists drew out the potential of his insights and made practices such as 'working-through' a method that could contribute to political transformation.

The path to healing in psychoanalysis, working-through is a process of excavating buried feelings, repressed experiences and internalised assumptions stored in the unconscious so they can be expressed in words and move into consciousness. In a feminist context, working-through might mean looking closely at the ways you've absorbed a system of patriarchal ideas, words and images premised on distorting your perspective and muting your voice. These limitations, and the feelings that exceed them, slip through cracks in the ego (the place where defences cohere) and manifest through your words. When listened to, these words become material for reflection with the potential for change. There is a poetics to this process, as representations of the self, once fixed, imaginatively attach to different images, words and sounds.

Working-through typically takes place on an individual scale between an analyst and patient, but Mulvey and Wollen projected the practice on screen with the hope that audiences might become feminist collectivities that challenge the suppression of women's voices and bring their differences into public life. Their many talks and public dialogues that accompanied screenings attest to their desire for the film's feminist argument to reach people. The collaboration between Mulvey and Wollen is the foundation of this process, and the production of the film, which brought activists, intellectuals and film-makers together, reflects the real possibility that avant-garde film-makers can pry open spaces in which people can come together to write new languages of desire.

1 The Directors' Address

Riddles is Mulvey and Wollen's second film. They made their first, *Penthesilea*: *Queen of the Amazons* (1974), in Evanston, Illinois, at Northwestern University's School of Radio, Film and Television. Wollen was teaching a graduate seminar on avant-garde cinema, and Paddy Whannel, with whom he worked in the BFI's Education Department, encouraged them to make a film with the equipment left unused during the holiday break. This 16mm film engages with Heinrich von Kleist's 1808 play about the myth of the Amazon Queen.

    Penthesilea foresees the feminist themes and formal experiments of *Riddles*. A 'film in five sequences', it is also organised as chapters that layer images, text and sound to excavate the stories buried in the images of the Amazons, described in the script as 'independent, aggressive and destructive'.[24] In the film's third sequence, Mulvey and Wollen present a series of art-historical objects that portray the Greeks sacking the Amazons. Ranging from classical antiquity to the late twentieth century, these aesthetic objects – sculptures, vases, shields, mosaics, bas reliefs, tapestries, paintings, illustrations, and finally, comics – depict battle scenes in which the aggression attributed to the Amazons is suppressed. Composed by Luciano Berio, an innovator in electronic music, and sung by Cathy Berberian, well known for her vocal experimentation, the score is full of distorted and visceral sounds – cries, moans, babbles, shrieks, laughs, whispers and howls. Set in relationship to images of entangled bodies frozen into choreographies of gendered violence, the score is an audible but incomprehensible language of women struggling to speak. Separated from the image track and pulsing at the edges of syntax and sense, these sounds represent the disruptive 'noise' long associated with women and can be heard as a cry for feminist collectivities.[25]

Penthesilea found an audience who could hear its collection of cries. In late 1974, Mulvey and Wollen moved back to London, and upon their return, they encountered the 'flourishing' of experimental and avant-garde film in Britain.[26] New collectives, festivals, clubs, screenings and publications – there was a utopian energy that brought film and left-wing politics together and emerged from the experimental film culture they had left behind.[27] Women's Liberation was part of this momentum. Screened at the Edinburgh International Film Festival in 1974, *Penthesilea* exemplified what feminist counter-cinema could do.

The film begins with a theatrical production of Kleist's play. Unfaithful to his script, they translated the play into a mime, which signals Mulvey and Wollen's expansive understanding of language. The Northwestern University Mime Company brought this version of *Penthesilea* to the stage, and it was shot in a high school auditorium in New Trier Township, Illinois. The actors coming together (even as warring Greeks and Amazons) links to their interest in film-making as a collective practice forged through friendships. Sider, a film student, edited *Penthesilea* and its soundtrack, and then moved to London to work on *Riddles*.

One clear connection to *Riddles* is *Penthesilea*'s second sequence in which Wollen addresses the audience and introduces the

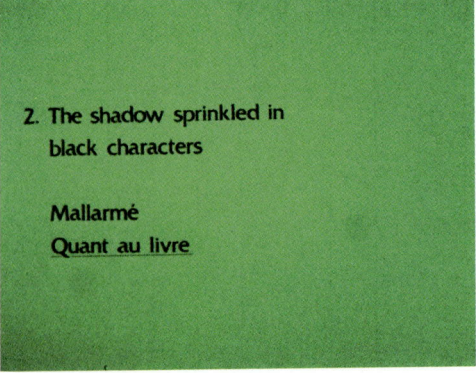

Penthesilea: Queen of the Amazons (1974)

Penthesilea: Queen of the Amazons

film as its director. An epigraph from Stéphane Mallarmé's 'Quant au livre' (1895) evokes ink and typography. In professorial mode, Wollen explains how *Penthesilea*, a 'montage film', differs from a 'normal narrative film'. Rather than relying on conventional editing to suture the cuts that compose an alternate world, their film is 'without editing', but nevertheless has 'discontinuities' and 'breaks'. Wollen's address to the audience is one of those breaks.

Tall and lanky, Wollen looks like the 1970s. He wears sunglasses (that never come off), a blue blazer with wide lapels (a microphone is clipped to one), a rose-coloured shirt and bell-bottoms. Moving around a garden room full of plants and natural light that streams in through high cathedral windows, Wollen reads from cue cards. He does not hide the fact that he is reading, and there is no attempt at naturalistic acting. Wollen tells the story of Penthesilea and Kleist's rewriting of it, which is distinct from legends and epics in one crucial respect. She kills Achilles. Kleist's revision is a point from which to examine fantasies of women – strong, aggressive, equal, fascinating, threatening, revolting – in the patriarchal imagination.

Throughout the sequence, Wollen leaves the cue cards on tables and chairs and among the leaves of the plants arranged around

Penthesilea: Queen of the Amazons

the set. Louis Castelli, a recent graduate of Northwestern, used a
handheld camera to focus on these fragments. While viewers read
Wollen's handwritten notes in capital letters, he is outside the frame
reading a different part of the script. This separation of image,
text and voice troubles the typical connections among authority,
knowledge and masculinity. Furthermore, Wollen's discussion of
the myth's feminist implications suggests the importance of men
working-through the patriarchal histories they inherit, benefit
from and often fight to keep in place, as the story of Penthesilea
demonstrates.

While *Penthesilea* showcases an address from a male director,
Riddles reflects Mulvey and Wollen's decision to emphasise a
woman's voice. They did so by first positioning Mulvey as the
director in the second chapter, 'Laura speaking', and secondly by
giving the Sphinx and her voice a prominent part. By 1977, a world
of feminist avant-garde film had begun to take hold, and this chapter
announces Mulvey's place in it. But 'Laura speaking' is not exactly
a representation of Mulvey 'herself'; the chapter is a performance in
which, as Wollen explains, a character named 'Laura' 'open[s]' 'the
symbolic role of author ... for female identification'.[28]

'Laura speaking' begins with an image from a Greek red-figure vase that portrays the Sphinx and Oedipus. The embattled characters are staring directly at each other. We hear Laura's voice before we see her, and she begins reflecting on their decision to make the Sphinx central to *Riddles*. Anticipating 'Louise's story told in thirteen shots', repeating the word 'voice' like a refrain, Mulvey explains:

> When we were planning the central section of the film, about a mother and a child, we decided to use the voice of the Sphinx as an imaginary narrator – because the Sphinx represents, not the voice of truth, not an answering voice, but its opposite: a questioning voice, a voice asking a riddle. The Oedipus myth associates the voice of the Sphinx with motherhood as mystery and with resistance to patriarchy.[29]

Associated with curiosity and uncertainty, the Sphinx will tell the story of the film's protagonist Louise. As the 'imaginary narrator', the Sphinx connects her struggles as a young working mother to the film's commitment to resisting patriarchal myths of motherhood.

In a fixed mid-range shot and against a black background, Mulvey sits at a small desk and reads from a text. For most of 'Laura speaking', she looks directly into the camera, but at first, she looks down at the text from which she reads. She places her

hands in an elegant pose that frames her face. Other portrayals
of the Sphinx – a black-figure oil flask in the British Museum's
collection; Gustave Moreau's 1864 oil painting *Oedipus and the
Sphinx* – appear in the first part of her exposition and illustrate
the museum world of Mulvey and Wollen's imagination. Mulvey
tells viewers about Oedipus, the most well-known literary figure
of psychoanalysis, and the Sphinx's forgotten role in his story:
'Everybody knows that Oedipus killed his father and married his
mother, but the part played by the Sphinx is often overlooked.' In
this measured manifesto, the erased memory of the Sphinx becomes

central to the film's argument about women's struggle to write their places into history.

'Laura speaking' is a portrait of the director and a still life arranged with small, everyday objects. They represent the effort to create a place – an address – from a woman's first-person perspective. Mulvey sits on a kitchen chair with worn edges and chipped paint. She wears a loosely fitting blouse with a floral pattern of fuchsia pink and pale green over a grey-green shirt. These sartorial details give this meditation on the voice of the Sphinx a bright sensuality and connect it to costume design, a form of work behind the scenes of film-making that historically women have been allowed to pursue. Arranged on the table are a microphone, spiral notebooks, a tape recorder, a child's enamel mug and a pencil sharpener in the form of a small globe. The bright blue of the globe pulls the greens and blues from Mulvey's fuchsia blouse to the foreground of the image, and the red cover of the spiral notebook and touches of red in the mug bring out its purples. These are early indications of the directors' use of colour to illuminate a rhythmic 'language' of visual sensations that overlaps with their attention to sound.

A scene of writing, 'Laura speaking' presents a woman taking up a position in space and a feminist voice coming into articulation. While Mulvey addresses her audience, she turns a green pencil in her

hands with nervous energy, as if she is going to give writing a new purpose. A still of Mulvey looking down at the pencil accompanied an interview conducted by the film critic Tony Rayns and published in *Time Out* to announce the premiere of *Riddles* at The Other Cinema on 13 May 1977.[30] The Other Cinema, an organisation established in 1969 to distribute avant-garde films from around the globe, opened a cinema on Tottenham Street in 1975.[31] Mulvey was on the advisory board of The Other Cinema, and in 'Laura speaking', she performs the work of distributing and screening feminist knowledge about the construction of 'woman' as 'other' (the difference through which 'man' recognises himself). Mayer notes its resemblance to a news broadcast, and with the desk, globe and static mid-range shot, this chapter stages a scene in which a woman makes an argument about the histories shaping women's everyday lives. 'Laura speaking' also materialises the hope they can speak with authority in public and actually be heard.[32]

For that to happen, however, the prestige of patriarchal masculinity had to be eroded, but Oedipus, Mulvey explains, was exceptional. Unlike the other men the Sphinx devoured, he solved her riddles. In response to this defeat, she killed herself. As Mulvey tells us this part of the story, the image of Garbo as the 'Sphinx Moderne' from *Midi-Minuit Fantastique* reappears. Like Napoleon's campaigns in Egypt at the beginning of the nineteenth century, which brought 'new life' to the myth of the Sphinx, the early twentieth-century cinema Garbo symbolises becomes another arena in which the Sphinx is 'disclosed once again to western eyes'.

Clarence Sinclair Bull, a still photographer for the major studios during Hollywood's Golden Age, created this surrealist portrait of Garbo as the Sphinx in 1931 and superimposed her face over an image of the Egyptian monument. As 'Sphinx Moderne', Garbo's image evokes the differences of sexuality and race. The still image hints at the androgyny of her persona and the suggestions of her lesbian sexuality, which connect to the Sphinx's fluid movement across gender and geography. While the Egyptian Sphinx was male, and the Greek Sphinx female, Mulvey argues that the Greek Sphinx can be 'projected' onto the 'blank face' of the Egyptian Sphinx as though it is a cinematic screen. Set against the sandy background of North Africa, the whiteness of Garbo's face – in his influential book *Mythologies* (1957), Roland Barthes describes it as a 'mask' and compares it to 'fragile and compact snow' – belies the neutrality attributed to Euro-American whiteness.[33] Garbo's pale face also illustrates bell hooks's point that images of 'ultra-white' Hollywood stars were produced to separate them from actresses of colour.[34] This distance, manufactured to make white femininity a distinct visual category, was part of an imperative that white actresses cover up, contain and reinforce the injustices of Hollywood's systemic racism – Mulvey calls it an 'apartheid' structure – and the images of racial difference it imprinted on the cultural imagination.[35] Collaged onto a photograph of the Sphinx, the image of Garbo narrows that distance.

A star of both silent film and the talkies, the icon of Garbo raises questions about the voice. Her 'white face' might be an anxious accompaniment to Al Jolson's 'black face' in the early talkie *The Jazz Singer* (1927), which links the appearance of the voice in cinema to racial appropriation. In Wollen's BFI Film Classic book devoted to *Singin' in the Rain* (1952) and its comedic portrayal of the transition to sound, he argues that to give this technological shift a 'happy ending', 'voice and image are naturally joined together'.[36] Synchronising images of women with their voices was the way to create this connection, but the Sphinx defies synchronisation. While there are images, like Garbo's face, to which it is linked, in *Riddles*, her voice is 'free-floating', beyond the visual world of the film, but also outside the visual economy of race, which fixes perceptions of physical characteristics to racial hierarchies.[37]

The Sphinx is an example of what Michel Chion identifies as the *acousmêtre*: a cinematic voice disconnected from an image of a body.[38] A rarity for cinematic portrayals of women, the voice of the Sphinx as *acousmêtre* displaces the demand to see the voice and image of a woman harmoniously aligned. As Kaja Silverman explains, the Sphinx 'escapes that anatomical destiny to which classic cinema holds its female characters'.[39] For feminist considerations of women and motherhood, a figure of this escape is crucial.

When Mulvey describes the Sphinx 'entering popular mythology', the film cuts to photographs of the Sphinx at Giza. The sandy grey Sphinx, majestic and broken, stares far off into the distance and its monumental dimensions stand out against the blue of the Egyptian sky. The pyramid of Khufu is in the background on the right, a geometric counterpoint to her immense physicality, which yokes strength to vulnerability on a colossal scale. For a few

minutes, the camera zooms in on her fractured visage. While these photographs are on screen, Mulvey solidifies the film's feminist argument about the Sphinx and discusses her as a figure of 'male fears and fantasies'. She is, as Mulvey explains, a 'cannibalistic mother, part bestial, part angelic, indecipherable'.

The Sphinx is a figure of the irrationality attributed to women. Opposed to the 'conscious mind' of Oedipus, she stands for the 'unconscious', and expresses women's 'sense of exclusion and suppression'. The point of *Riddles*, Mulvey tells us, is to rewrite the histories in which woman is conflated with the irrational disorder of the unconscious and repressed by the rational order associated with masculinity. While the Sphinx is 'a threat and a riddle', Mulvey counters that this is a projection, as 'women within patriarchy are faced with a never-ending series of threats and riddles – dilemmas which are hard for women to solve, because the culture within which they must think is not theirs'. When Mulvey says this, there is a sadness in her voice that gives her address a melancholic cast.

Concluding her soliloquy, Mulvey returns to motherhood: 'We live in a society ruled by the father, in which the place of motherhood is suppressed. Motherhood and how to live it, or not live it, lies at the root of the dilemma.' Prying apart their conflation in patriarchal cultures, the link between woman and motherhood is a puzzle the film tries to solve. Desire is the key, and the directors wrote the voice of the Sphinx to provoke viewers into reflecting on the desires for maternal care projected onto images of women that limit their range and complexity. As Mulvey states: 'And meanwhile, the Sphinx can only speak with a voice apart, a voice off.' Without a visible source, a 'voice-off' is an alternative to the 'voice-over', the familiar technique for representing a character's subjective perspective and establishing a film's meaning. While her voice is outside the frame, the Sphinx is central. She guides Louise's story as she brings the value and pleasure of maternal care into public life.

2 Writing the Voice of the Sphinx

'Laura speaking' tells us *Riddles* is an essay film. Sprung from
the literary essay and the self-reflection it enables, essay films are
speculative cinematic experiments that often combine fiction and
documentary. (In French, '*essayer*' means 'to try'.) The genre began
to take hold in the 1920s with Eisenstein's proposal to direct a
film version of Karl Marx's *Capital* (1867).[40] After slowly gaining
momentum in the twentieth century, the essay film did not become a
salient genre until the twenty-first.[41] When Mulvey and Wollen made
Riddles in 1977, they thought of it as a 'theoretical' film.[42] The fact
that *Riddles* aligns so well with the essay film before it was widely
recognised highlights the visionary dimensions of their film-making.

   Mulvey and Wollen's feminist critique of a culture that overlooks
the Sphinx links to the essay film's resistance to dominant perceptions.
As Nora M. Alter explains, essay films often interrupt 'accepted ways
of viewing and understanding the world'.[43] Deliberately porous, essay
films solicit viewers to co-create unfamiliar ways of seeing. The voice
is a primary material for bringing critique and audience participation
together, as the disjunct between voice and image typical of the essay
film can create, as Alter puts it, a 'jarring collision of opposites and
complex levels of meaning that spectators must disentangle and
co-produce in their own way'.[44] In this 'collision', sound does not
support the image but moves along its own track. This separation
creates an 'alternative to visual spectacle' and, in turn, 'free[s] the
viewer's imagination from the constraints of the visible world'.[45]
Focused on women, the predominant symbols of 'visual spectacle',
Riddles enacts the challenging process of freeing the imagination.

   To make the Sphinx into a figure who attests to the 'constraints
of the visible world' and transforms them, Mulvey and Wollen
draw on the connection between writing and film-making at the

heart of the genre. In 1948, Alexandre Astruc, an early theorist of the essay film, developed the concept of the '*caméra-stylo*' (camera pen). According to Astruc, the '*caméra-stylo*' will 'break free from the tyranny of what is visual'.[46] Beginning with the layering of texts in 'Opening pages', Mulvey and Wollen highlight the *graph* in 'cinematography' and show that in *Riddles*, film-making is a 'form of inscription', not 'a capture and reproduction of the world'.[47] Writing with the camera, Mulvey and Wollen inscribe fissures in dominant images to excavate the voices buried within them.

This writerly aesthetic connects to Mulvey and Wollen's investment in psychoanalysis. They followed the idea, evident throughout Freud's oeuvre, that writing accesses unconscious feelings and fantasies, and made it into a tool for feminist exploration. The cinematic writing in *Riddles* leads to the historical memories and unconscious myths that keep patriarchal values intact. One of these myths is that women are, or should be, silent, stifled under masculinist authority, letting its dominance move through women's voices without restraint. Rather than bypassing the histories that have narrowed the full range of women's expression, *Riddles* writes a visual letter to viewers and invites them to collectively work-through the psychically sedimented ways in which women's personal experiences have been exiled from the visibility of public speech.

All paths lead to writing in Mulvey and Wollen's collaboration. There are the scripts they wrote together. Rich with poetic experiment, they collage an array of literary genres, and do so, as Oliver Fuke notes, in 'singular and novel ways'.[48] The scripts are creative extensions of three influential essays that foresaw *Riddles*: Mulvey's 'Visual Pleasure and Narrative Cinema' and Wollen's 'Godard and Counter-Cinema: *Vent d'Est*' (1972) and 'The Two Avant-Gardes' (1975). These texts assert their feminist commitments to intervening in Hollywood cinema, on the one hand, and the avant-garde film movement on the other. Though eventually they worked in university film departments, Mulvey and Wollen did not write these essays for academic audiences. Nor were they composed as regular pieces of film criticism. They are theoretical manifestos of two activist-intellectuals becoming film-makers.

'Visual Pleasure' is the essay to which Mulvey's name will always be attached. Published in the British film journal *Screen*, it is usually read in isolation, detached from her work as a director and her collaboration with Wollen. Marking her break with Hollywood, the central concept of 'Visual Pleasure' is the 'male gaze', a way of perceiving and using women exclusively for their visual and sexual appeal. The essay stands at the beginning of feminist film theory, a body of scholarship with two interrelated purposes: examining how the history of film has contributed to the subordination of women and revealing how feminist film-making can subvert that history. Once hotly debated, Mulvey has revisited, revised and deepened her account of the 'male gaze' many times throughout her career. It is now a familiar part of talking about sexism in visual culture.

'Visual Pleasure' focuses on Hollywood films produced from the early 1930s to the mid-1960s, the period that loosely encompasses the rise and fall of the studio system: Josef von Sternberg's *Morocco* (1930), Howard Hawks's *Only Angels Have Wings* (1939) and *To Have and Have Not* (1944), and Alfred Hitchcock's *Rear Window* (1954), *Vertigo* (1958) and *Marnie* (1964). The coherent world of these cinematic narratives, in which Mulvey was absorbed during her days as a cinephile, relies on images of women frozen into an erotically charged subservience that soothes Oedipal figures behind the camera, on screen and in the audience. Performances of feminine beauty tell masculine-identified viewers they are rightfully placed at the centre of the narrative action – the 'I' at the beginning, middle and end of the story.

Mulvey draws on psychoanalysis to demonstrate how Hollywood film links patriarchal desires for mastery to unconscious desires. She utilises Freud's concepts scopophilia (erotically charged looking), fetishisation (substituting desired body parts for whole people) and castration (the threat of losing the penis and the power bestowed upon it), but she does not take them at face value. Instead,

Mulvey redeploys them as 'political weapon[s]' to identify how the superiority granted masculinity, and the subordination of women that guarantees it, become embedded in the language of Hollywood film.[49] This language allows the masculine-identified subject to avoid a confrontation with the unconscious, where his hold on masculinity is radically unstable.

Images are the primary focus of 'Visual Pleasure', but the voice is implicated in the picture of femininity Mulvey diagnoses. She draws on the work of the French psychoanalyst Jacques Lacan and his argument that language – the system of laws and conventions he calls the Symbolic Order – is the means by which men access verbal authority. The Symbolic triumphs over the mirroring associated with maternal care, a realm Lacan calls the Imaginary. Deploying this argument without taking it as a truth, Mulvey argues that in Classic Hollywood cinema, the masculine-identified viewer can 'live out his fantasies and obsessions through linguistic command by imposing them on the silent image of woman still tied to her place as bearer, not maker, of meaning'.[50] Her choice of the word 'bearer', which evokes women's reproductive capacities and the responsibilities attached to them, highlights the presumption that women hold, nurture and mirror others. This 'bearing' muffles women and prevents them from becoming 'maker[s] of meaning', a phrase that captures the agency of the director and his power to arrange a film's images and sounds. As the 'imaginary narrator', the Sphinx interrupts this gendered division of labour and reveals its implications for women's voices.

Wollen's 'Godard and Counter-Cinema' and 'The Two Avant-Gardes' do not engage with feminism or psychoanalysis as Mulvey does in 'Visual Pleasure'. But when these three essays are read in dialogue, it is clear Wollen identified the tools the directors would use in *Riddles* to unearth women's voices from the visual language of commercial cinema.

In 'Godard and Counter-Cinema', Wollen charts how the French-Swiss director created 'revolutionary' and 'materialist'

counterpoints to Hollywood film.[51] Originally published in
Afterimage, a journal started in response to the student protests
that took place in 1968 at the University of Essex, the essay is
a lexicon of the techniques Godard developed for challenging
cinematic orthodoxy, many of which make their way into *Riddles*:
the chapters that interrupt the expectation of a cohesive story; the
opaque portrayal of character; the direct address; the use of text
and typography to block transparency; the film within a film; the
quotation of shots by other directors; the rejection of naturalistic
acting. Godard wrote about films before becoming a director, and
Wollen stresses how he brought a writer's attention to language into
his films, making it the always shifting material of his heterogeneous
worlds. Godard's engagement with texts to separate voice and
character and deflect identification was particularly important for
Mulvey and Wollen. They used it to write the voice of the Sphinx.

These strategies reveal Godard's debts to Bertolt Brecht, the
German communist, playwright and theorist who engaged with the
innovations of the Soviet avant-garde for his work in the 1930s. As
'Godard and Counter-Cinema' makes clear, Godard brought Brecht's
Verfremdungseffekt (typically translated as 'alienation technique')
to cinema to interrupt its hallucinatory power, and yet like Brecht,
he did not dismiss the pleasure revolutionary cinema requires for
its dreams and fantasies. Wollen helped to bring both Brecht's work
and the Soviet avant-garde to the pages of *Screen* in the early 1970s,
which underscores the revolutionary stakes of his collaborations
with Mulvey.

Published in a special issue of *Studio International: Journal of
Modern Art* devoted to 'Avant-Garde Film in England and Europe',
Wollen's essay 'The Two Avant-Gardes' builds upon his work in *Signs
and Meaning in the Cinema* (1969), in the BFI's Cinema One series.[52]
This field-defining book establishes an expansive definition of film –
in dialogue with aesthetic theory, other arts, popular media and
vernacular forms of cultural expression – but also draws on semiotics
(the study of how signs, split between the signifier and signified,

create meaning) to identify film as a specific aesthetic language. Displaying his talent for mapping the historical patterns of aesthetic movements, in 'The Two Avant-Gardes', Wollen outlines the two primary camps of radical film-makers in the 1960s and early 1970s: the Anglo-American Co-op movement – he gestures to Peter Gidal (an American expat), Malcolm Le Grice and Stephen Dwoskin (also an American expat) – and the directors working in Europe, such as Godard and the team of Jean-Marie Straub and Danièle Huillet. The former created experimental meditations on film as a visual medium, and the latter composed political arguments by reassembling language, discourse and narratives.[53]

As Wollen notes, Co-op film-makers rejected narrative, and by working with the components of film – printing, mirroring, projection, focus and camera angles – produced lyrical meditations on the forms of sight the medium makes possible. Co-op films attest to the impact of art schools on film-making, and Wollen identifies Cubist films of the 1920s, like those made by Man Ray and László Moholy-Nagy, as their predecessors. The Co-op film-makers were also in dialogue with the New American Cinema Group, film-makers such as Stan Brakhage, Hollis Frampton and Michael Snow, who made exposing the devices of cinema their subject.

While the Co-op group explored the signifiers of film, its optical textures and physical forms, the second group, drawing heavily from literature and theatre, focused on historical signifieds, the production of historical meaning. For example, Straub–Huillet's 1972 film *Geschichtsunterricht* (*History Lessons*) builds upon Brecht's unfinished novel *Die Geschäfte des Herrn Julius Caesar* (*The Business Affairs of Mr Julius Caesar*). It begins with a drive through contemporary Rome and maps that depict the shrinking Roman Empire. Wollen claims these directors produced their most revolutionary work in 1968 and struggled with the imperative to make a political impact by reaching audiences. They are descendants, Wollen argues, of the Soviet directors Eisenstein and Dziga Vertov, who, while forging the language of film, were faithful to historical content. Between these two avant-gardes, Wollen saw an 'alternative route' in Godard's *Le Gai savoir* (1969).[54] This film is, according to Wollen, 'about the possibility of meaning itself, of generating new types of meaning', a pursuit the two groups shared.[55]

Rejecting purity, Mulvey and Wollen drew from both avant-gardes in *Riddles* to 'generat[e] new' and particularly feminist 'types of meaning'. In 'Laura speaking', they borrowed from the film-makers invested in politics and history to address the position of women in western culture. In 'Stones', the chapter to which I now turn, they reveal their debts to the Co-op film-makers. Their investigation of film as a medium encouraged Mulvey and Wollen to delve into the cinematic image and begin writing the voice of the Sphinx from its depths.

3 The Sounds of the Longest Revolution

At the end of 'Laura speaking', Mulvey plaintively states, 'the Sphinx can only speak in a voice apart, a voice off'. The word 'off' works like a switch. A turquoise-blue '3' appears, and the third chapter, 'Stones', begins. Before we see images, there is an eruption of cool and high-pitched sounds. Though dense, these sounds seems to flutter over travel footage that moves swiftly across the Egyptian landscape as if shot from a train. This is the first time we are hearing music. A dramatic introduction to the film's score, it unfolds in quick swirls.

The score was composed by Mike Ratledge. A classically trained musician, Ratledge was part of Canterbury's progressive music scene, and in 1966, he founded Soft Machine with four other musicians. Soft Machine was a jazz-rock fusion band known for its psychedelic soundscapes collaged together from an experimental array of musical genres and styles. A songwriter, organist and keyboardist influenced by Cecil Taylor, Ratledge linked stream-of-consciousness improvisation with complex compositional structures.[56] In the 1970s, Ratledge brought the synthesiser into Soft Machine's orchestrations.

Denys Irving, who designed the multi-track synthesisers upon which Ratledge performed the score for *Riddles*, recommended him to the directors.[57]

Mulvey and Wollen were not prescriptive. They began talking to Ratledge before production started and were open to his interpretations. As a result, the score provokes viewers' subjective engagement rather than dictating emotional responses. Now a stand-alone album, it is connected to but also distinct from the film. The synthesiser's electronically generated vibrations – heard by the ear as music – give the score a futuristic sci-fi feel, but it also seems haunted by the past. The modal patterns suggest well-worn histories in which women's voices were suppressed as unruly noise. Sider recalls that because 16mm has a narrow band of frequencies, the high and low registers of Ratledge's composition could not be heard, which is perhaps the reason the notes seem to bounce against their edges.[58]

For 'Stones', Ratledge creates metallic flurries with quick tempos that he layers over drowsy, anachronistic sounds. These sounds form a simple pattern that is the chapter's sonic foundation. He also plays the melodies in a minor key, which creates a slightly sad affect. Tracking its imaginative movement through time and across geographies, Mayer notes that the score is an 'electronic transport between ancient Greece, ancient Egypt, European colonial wars in the Middle East, and the present day', historical dimensions that enhance the hazy images of the Sphinx and the pyramids.[59] These images have a soft blue tint and look to be suffused in the pale pinks of the desert sand. Footage of tourists on horseback and postcard kiosks punctuate the film with warm reds. A shadowy image of a horse makes 'Stones' feel like a memory of a dream.

The camera slowly zooms in on the images of the Sphinx's face, mouth and lips, carved from stone and permanently closed. Eroded, marked by fractures and missing pieces, this stoic portrait is an image of the 'dark continent', Freud's metaphor for the mysteries of femininity. Borrowed from explorer Henry Morton Stanley's

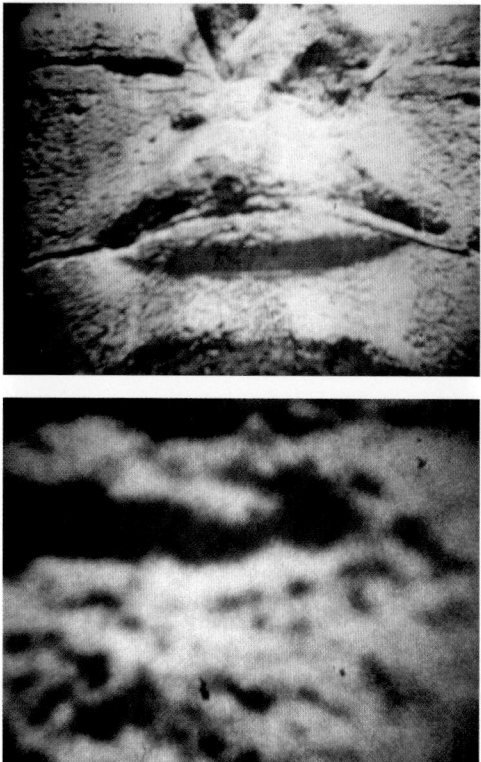

description of Africa, the 'dark continent' relies on the racial
hierarchies of European colonialism to identify what is 'primitive'
about women and what is feminised about those designated 'dark'
and racially other to Euro-American whiteness. Moving through
these layers of the colonial imaginary, the camera expresses the
desire to get as close to the Sphinx as possible, to hear what she has
been barred from saying. While the stone of the monument makes
that suppression final, the music seems to animate the possibility of
speech. The closer the camera gets, the more iconoclastic the chapter
becomes. The images disintegrate into the grain of the celluloid

film and become abstract textures that correspond with the score's pulsating sounds. Still, the lips do not part; the images do not speak; a voice has yet to emerge.

'Stones' reflects the directors' dialogue with the London Film-makers' Co-op and its commitment to the material and processes of making films. Of the two 'avant-gardes' featured in Wollen's essay, this Co-op was established in 1966 and fostered a communal, anti-capitalist and anti-establishment ethos for British cinema. Echoing the flaws of Co-op films, the found footage in 'Stones' is scratched, faded and marked by dust, tactile qualities that evoke the feeling of time passing.

Mulvey and Wollen fed their footage through a motion-analysis projector, which is used to slow down moving images and focus on details that elude the human eye. (They are typically used in sports and criminal investigations.) They borrowed the projector from Marc Karlin of the Berwick Street Film Collective, the group who made the avant-garde documentary *Nightcleaners* (1975), which portrays the women who cleaned London office buildings at night, raised children during the day and organised for better working conditions. To deepen the textures of the images, Mulvey and Wollen also projected the footage on the wall and began a process of refilming the screened images.[60] This process erodes the images so the crevices of the stone and the grain of the celluloid seem to merge.

The filigreed sounds of Ratledge's score contribute to this disintegration. With its puzzling, hard-to-identify affects, the music encourages the kind of listening that psychoanalysis fosters, one that tunes into what cannot be said but listeners can nevertheless hear and feel. The quick tempos are restless, slightly crazed. In her reflections on film's shift to synchronised sound in the 1920s, Mulvey writes that the voice is on the 'cusp between resonance and significance', as it is part of the 'material texture' of a soundtrack, but as the vehicle of speech, it also relays content and meaning.[61] The voice of the Sphinx is on this cusp, and the music of 'Stones' allows it to waver there as a medium of film before coming into articulation.

> **Perhaps Louise is too close to her child. How much longer can she reject the outside world, other people and other demands? Her husband often**

The third chapter, 'Louise's story', works-through the silence the stone monument embodies and continues to bring its latent poetry to the surface of the cinematic image. Before the first 360-degree pan of 'Louise's story' begins, there is a poetic fragment in turquoise-blue lettering against an inky black background. Recalling the intertitles of silent films, this fragment is an incomplete glimpse into the story.

These words register the gaze of the outside world and replicate the ease with which maternal care is scrutinised. The clock is ticking for Louise; her relationship with her two-year-old daughter Anna is considered too close. The line breaks fracture the story and suggest notes and interrupted thoughts. By cutting off the last sentence, Mulvey and Wollen invite viewers to fill in what is left unsaid. The text is suspended in uncertainty, but if Louise has rejected the 'outside / world, other people and other / demands', this rejection likely includes '[h]er husband'. It seems the missing verb would express his disappointment.

As the intertitle fades, Ratledge's score begins again and the camera depicts three cobalt-blue cooking pots with silver rims. This first pan takes place in Louise's kitchen and evokes a world she has created by taking care of Anna, dense with the colours and textures of domestic objects. This is a world that resonates with the mother's importance but 'other people' expect her to leave. Slow and steady,

the camerawork defies the expectation that Louise should hurry up and relinquish that centrality to re-establish the father's authority.

A domestic still life as a cinematic *mise en scène*, the first objects of the shot establish its intricate patterns. In front of the blue cooking pots are a yellow plastic bowl and a pale blue towel embroidered with pink and yellow flowers and tiny green leaves. These objects have been placed on a pale grey kitchen counter and before a wall decorated with wallpaper. Grey, white and black, the intricate lines and shapes of the wallpaper's arabesque design bring another pattern to the scene. The wallpaper rhymes with the silver accents of the pots and contributes to the vivid density of the blues, yellows and greens.

Creating patterns from a narrow palette of notes, the sounds of Ratledge's synthesiser float through the scene without impetus or direction. These sonic qualities contribute to the portrayal of everyday routines and tasks. As Louise moves around the kitchen preparing breakfast for Anna, she crosses the field of vision in a seemingly haphazard fashion and the sounds become part of the attention the scene pays to the affective texture of domestic objects – and Louise's desire to stay among them.

Ratledge composed the music for this pan with three chords that give it a lyrical tone, upbeat but also elongated, a slow reverie.

Aligned with but also distinct from the pans, the patterns Ratledge arranges are extradiegetic (outside the world of the film), but it feels like they are coming from inside this intimate space. The music stands in for the conversation between mother and daughter but keeps the closeness of their relationship enclosed in privacy. It also contributes to a sense of confinement, as there are no windows in Louise's kitchen. Indirectly, Louise's attachment to Anna may represent the constraints placed on women, and the score's repetitions evoke feelings of claustrophobia.

The camera moves clockwise, which connects it to the movement of time and reading. We do not see Louise's face. Instead, consistent with the detached acting style of *Riddles*, the camera is positioned to circle through the middle of the kitchen and at waist level. We see Louise's torso as she holds Anna, wipes her hands, her scruffy brown teddy bear (which actually belonged to Tise) and her own shirt. The work she performs with her hands comes into view. Louise points to the embroidered flowers on another towel, which suggests she is teaching Anna words. After Louise puts her into her highchair and gives her pieces of apples to eat, the little girl mimes the care of feeding and talks to her teddy bear. Anna happily addresses her mother, opening her mouth in glee. Outside the frame, Louise is the 'acoustic mirror', Silverman's term for the maternal figure who recognises the child with her voice and holds her within it, creating a sensuous envelope with sound. The shot also illustrates Silverman's point that mothers often are 'the first language teacher[s]' who 'organize the world linguistically' for their children.[62]

The camera moves across a white door with a silver door handle. We finally hear the voice of the Sphinx. She speaks in phrases strung together through lyrical repetitions.

> Time to get ready. Time to come in.
> Things to forget. Things to lose.
> Meal time. Story time.

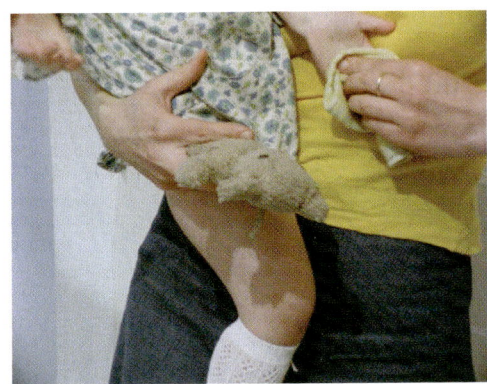

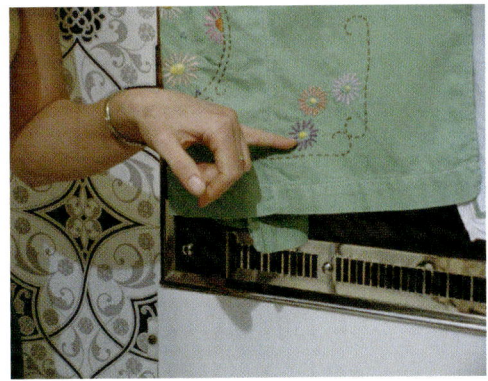

Moving past the concern raised in the intertitle that it is time for Louise to let go of Anna, the word 'time' becomes more than a temporal measurement. It is now a ringing sound and a 'thing' to 'forget' and 'lose'. These lines also connect the film's book-like structure – 'Story time' – to the work Louise performs in the kitchen – 'Meal time'.

The voice of the Sphinx is unabashedly feminine. Maddox brought dulcet tones and a soft, high pitch to her portrayal. Since masculinist cultures are generally averse to voices that register as feminine, this choice is an act of feminist defiance. It challenges phobias about the female body, women and femininity. One might assume that the Sphinx will sound differently as the story of Louise's relationship to feminism unfolds, but her voice remains the same. Rather than giving it the low-pitched sounds associated with masculine strength and authority, Mulvey and Wollen ask viewers to change how they hear femininity.

As the camera continues around the kitchen, it sculpts a tapestry of domestic objects: a hanging calendar with recipes for the month of September; towels and aprons; a radio; a lime-green decorative plate painted with small flowers; a yellow melon and three green apples on a plate reflected in the mirror of a steel toaster (another allusion to the still-life tradition). As it turns on its orderly course, the camera gives each domestic object it comes across the same magical vibration.

Entwined from the start, the clothing Louise and Anna wear – a solid lemon-yellow shirt and blue skirt and a cotton dress with a floral pattern of light blues and greens, respectively – deepens the attention to texture, touch and colour. Mulvey writes that they chose a fixed focal length and film with a slow speed to give the colours their bright saturation.[63] The camera portrays Louise cracking and whisking eggs in a white ceramic bowl decorated with bold stripes of cobalt blue. These stripes of blue, like lines in a poem that create a pattern across the page of the image, will repeat when we see the rows of clean bowls and plates in a blue dish rack. Domestic labour becomes an aesthetic practice – more than a set of tasks to complete.

To generate the poetry the Sphinx recites, Wollen drew on the chance procedures of the early twentieth-century French writer Raymond Roussel. Roussel composed poems by transforming a common phrase into a series of words with similar sounds, allowing the acoustic dimension of language to spill from sense and guide the poem's composition.

Idolise. Tranquilise.
Losing count. Losing control.
Shaking like a leaf. Release.
Things to say.

The poetry of *Riddles* resembles free association, a primary tool in psychoanalysis for working-through. It links the everyday life of Louise to the world of dreams, where linear time does not apply. But time is crucial to both cooking and making films, and Stabb had to finish scrambling the eggs as the pan (pun intended) concluded its course. Similarly, the clock of production needs to keep moving so a film will not go over budget. Keith Griffiths, an associate producer on the BFI Production Board, kept things on schedule.[64] Within *Riddles*, however, there is resistance to the realities of linear time, as it is linked to the rational order associated with patriarchal masculinity.

When the pan concludes, we see the torso of Louise's husband, Chris (Clive Merrison), in a brown tweed jacket holding a folded newspaper (representing the historical time of the outside world) and snatching a few pieces of toast cut for Anna. He is an afterthought. Later we learn Chris is a film-maker. His presence raises questions about the place of men in Women's Liberation, and perhaps Wollen's role in the film's feminist argument. Wollen described his and Mulvey's films as 'interrogations of language itself, symbolic quests in search of the place from which women could utter repressed counter-meanings of patriarchal discourse'.[65] Can men relinquish the voice of authority and open spaces in which women can 'utter' these 'counter-meanings'?

Wollen's writing opened these spaces by engaging with the work of feminist thinkers who made language an object of enquiry and a site of contestation. One of those thinkers is Julia Kristeva. A practising psychoanalyst, Kristeva's work brings semiotics, feminism and psychoanalysis together to reveal how the pulsating rhythms of music, art and poetry offer access to the differences of women's bodily experiences (inscribed by patriarchy's long histories) and the significance of maternal care.

In the first pan, we can see Mulvey and Wollen's engagement with Kristeva's concept of the 'chora', a rich and sensuous place of pre-verbal orality. Arising from the intersubjective loop of infant care, the chora is the bodily source of vocal music, rhythm and colour. The mother sculpts the chora by tuning into the expressive rhythms of the infant's bodily needs.[66] It is a container that holds the poetry of sensation before the child situates herself in the syntax of rational order and the laws written by patriarchal history.[67] As the child develops, she loses the chora to the unconscious. However, as an adult, she can access it through loving a child, fantasising or responding to the sounds, colours and textures of art.

The preparatory notes for the film highlight the directors' attention to colour. In the drawings for the first pan in the kitchen, Wollen made notes of the colours in writing: 'black & white patterns on walls', and in corresponding blue ink, 'blue towel rack', 'blue saucepans', 'silver, blue & white utensils'.[68] Blue runs like a ribbon through *Riddles*. It reflects the film's Egyptian themes – the first synthetic blue was invented in Egypt when the Great Pyramids were built in 2200 BC – as well as its focus on a child's psychic development. In her reflections on the 'luminous blue' of the thirteenth-century painter Giotto, Kristeva follows blue, which has the shortest wavelength of all the colours, to the edge of visual form and perception.[69] Similar to the sonic envelope created by the maternal voice, blue immerses us in a dimension of vision before infants fully recognise themselves in language and as discrete images. The colour is a 'zone' where identity 'vanishes'.[70] In *Riddles*, blue

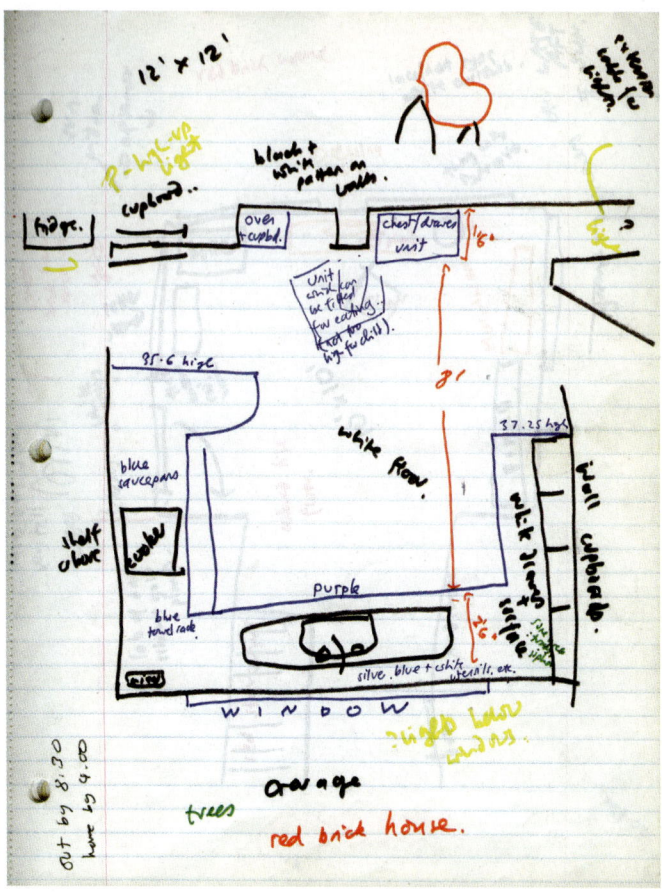

Peter Wollen's drawing for the first 360-degree panning shot in Chapter 4, 'Louise's story told in thirteen shots': Louise's kitchen, c. 1977 (© Laura Mulvey)

evokes the tender care of holding the bodies of children and placing them in the world's arrangement of space and time.

Intricate and slow, the first pan also corresponds to what feminist activist, writer and psychoanalyst Juliet Mitchell identified in 1966 as the 'longest revolution'. A foundational text for

Women's Liberation in Britain, in 'Women: The Longest Revolution', Mitchell seeks to understand the specific origin of women's oppression. She works within and against classic texts in Marxist and socialist thought to identify the places where beliefs about women's inferiority are naturalised as facts. According to Mitchell, there are four components of women's material conditions that determine their secondary status: 'Production, Reproduction, Sex and Socialization of children'.[71] These are the factors that need to transform for a feminist revolution to take place, and the family is part of each one. Shrouded in idealisation, assumed to be universal, the family makes the project of women's emancipation long and difficult.

The kitchen is the place where families are nurtured and women's oppression is sustained. Other feminist artists and film-makers situated their work in the kitchen and composed grim reflections on domesticity's restraints. There is Martha Rosler's performance video *Semiotics of the Kitchen* (1975) and Chantal Akerman's *Jeanne Dielman, 23 quai du Commerce, 1080 Bruxelles* (1975), a revolutionary feminist film that, for Mulvey, opened cinema to the time and space of women's work.[72] *Riddles* is in dialogue with these kitchens, but it is also evoking something different – a woman's sensuous awakening to sounds, colours and textures to rewrite the low value attributed to domestic labour.

Louise's kitchen highlights the 'homemade' aesthetic created by collectives of artists and film-makers who came together in the late 1960s and 1970s. They filmed this shot in the home of Malcolm and Judith Le Grice, at 10 Buckingham Road. Malcolm was a key figure in the London Film-makers' Co-op. He began his career as a painter, and many of his films, full of colour, light and sound, look like abstract paintings moving in time. Le Grice made specific features of the medium, such as film strips and sprocket holes, the source of his imagery. He also embraced the vernacular iterations of film-making, like the home movie, and transformed their flaws and patterns into visual poems.

The 360-degree pans are crucial to the film's meditation on skill, artistry, gender and domestic labour. They were executed by the cinematographer Diane Tammes. Tammes shot *Riddles* with an Éclair NPR (noiseless portable reflex), a 16mm sync sound camera. These light, portable and inexpensive cameras were important for both underground film and *cinéma vérité* style.[73] Feminist film-makers made their range of movement a tool for resisting the expectations that images of women will remain in place.

Although the Éclair NPR was handheld, Tammes mounted hers on a Moy gearhead (a kind of tripod) that had both a pan and a tilt handle. This allowed Tammes to decide on the angle of the shot and lock it in place. Mulvey stresses how indispensable Tammes was to the creation of the pans: 'It was Diane's combination of knowledge, ingenuity and imagination that enabled this aesthetic strategy to be realised in practice.'[74] She built platforms of wood and brick to hold the camera equipment, which allowed her to move it steadily while turning the handle.

Tammes is both outside and inside the 360-degree pans she executed for *Riddles*. Her technical skill put her in control of the *mise en scène*. At the same time, Tise, the little girl who plays Anna, is her daughter. Filming her child in a scene about the pleasures of domesticity, Tammes creates a feminist gaze with maternal care at its source.

Mulvey and Wollen were determined to hire a woman as their cinematographer, which in 1977 was rare.[75] Through a mutual friend, they heard about Tammes, a woman who started her career working as a still photographer for theatres in Scotland and had recently graduated from the National Film and Television School. She became the first woman accredited by the Association of Cinematograph, Television and Allied Technicians (ACTT). Because of her membership, the association changed the grade (job title and category) from 'cameraman' to 'cameraperson', which connects Tammes to the feminist media activism that arose from this organisation.[76] Describing the challenges of her training,

Tammes writes that it took a long time to 'acquire the dexterity to be unselfconscious', but stresses that the 'hardest task of all was just to feel I was talented and courageous enough to persist'.[77]

In 1973, the ACTT investigated the 'patterns of discrimination' women experienced in the film and television industry. They found that women worked in 'lower grade' jobs that required fewer technical skills, earned less and held little authority. Intertwined perceptions about the family justified this discrimination. Men were considered the 'breadwinners' and women's work in the industry was perceived to be secondary to their primary occupation as mothers (whether they were mothers or not). The union published their findings in 1975.[78] Just a year later, workers at the Grunwick Film Processing Laboratories, many of them South Asian women recently expelled from Uganda, went on strike and demanded union representation. These interventions connect to Mulvey's interest in the link between the images of women on screen – bearing the meaning of male fantasy in the glow of the spotlight – and the inequities they face if they are allowed to get behind the scenes, making the images, but hidden from view.[79] Tammes's camerawork bridges and attenuates these mutually reinforcing exploitations.

Other feminist directors hired women as their cinematographers. In the US, the avant-garde feminist film-maker Yvonne Rainer worked with Babette Mangolte, the cinematographer for Akerman's *Jeanne Dielman* who would later work with Sally Potter on *The Gold Diggers* (1983). In her recent reflections on the historical shift in which women film-makers have 'accumulated momentum', Mulvey writes, 'when women make films, cinema mutates in their hands and through their eyes'.[80]

The next shot of 'Louise's story' continues to pay attention to the hands and eyes of women. Set in the directors' home at 207 Ladbroke Grove, Louise moves across Anna's nursery, 'tidying up', as it says in the fragment that precedes the shot, and arranges the girl's things – dolls, puzzles, books, drawings, tea sets, doll's houses, hanging mobiles, photographs of animals, a chalkboard with a clock.

These toys are figures for the play of film-making. As Tammes circles
the camera at the height of Anna's cot, we see Louise bent at the waist
and putting back pieces of a puzzle that depicts jobs for girls and
boys. The scene highlights a mother's artistry composing worlds that
hold a child's attachments (as well as her own). A lullaby with deep
and low sounds, Ratledge's music conjures the twilight of bedtime,
its proximity to dreams. The poetry the Sphinx recites tips into the
unconscious content of family life – 'breast', '[b]leeding' and 'incest' –
and links it to exploitation – '[d]ispossessed', 'subject to conquest'.

A reproduction of Mary Cassatt's *Woman with a Sunflower* (*c.*
1905) highlights maternal care as a valued aesthetic project. Placed on
a purple piece of cardboard among snapshot photographs, the image
of Cassatt's painting portrays a white woman helping a child sitting on
her lap to hold up a handheld mirror trimmed with gold. The child's
reflection is a little portrait that overlaps painting and maternal care.
Pinned to the mother's dress is a sunflower, a symbol of the suffrage
movement. Its bright yellows echo the toys. Pollock argues that
Impressionist painters such as Cassatt utilised pictorial compression
to portray bourgeois white women enclosed within domestic spaces.
By doing so, they drew attention to femininity's codes of confinement,
but also women's embodied experiences of such spaces, which were
not exclusively oppressive and rich with sensation.[81] Indirectly, the

paintings of women Impressionists demonstrate that white middle-class women were, for the most part, barred from the public spaces their male contemporaries could frequent with impunity – like bars and brothels – as men were granted the freedom to move through the urban underworld and its proximity to the underclass without being sullied by shame. Replicating the spatial production of white femininity while also creating slim openings for seeing the gaze of the female spectator, the women in Cassatt's paintings are closed within, complicit with and mostly sequestered from the imperial exploits of the US and France and the hierarchies of class and race they solidified. While *Riddles* takes place in the 1970s, this multi-sensory film suggests that Louise has been moved to rewrite these visual scripts of confinement, pull out their dense pleasures and join her voice to the sounds of the longest revolution.

Mary Cassatt, *Woman with a Sunflower* (c. 1905)
(Chester Dale Collection, National Portrait Gallery)

4 Feminism's Collective Voice

As 'Louise's story' continues, the pans expand, more of London in the 1970s comes into the frame and the connections between *Riddles* and Women's Liberation become clearer. In the shots at the centre of this chapter, Mulvey and Wollen portray the effects of collective practices that gave women permission to work-through internalised silences and begin speaking through feminism's collective voice.

One of these practices was consciousness-raising: a collaborative process of naming, describing and sharing experiences women thought to be theirs alone, but were actually the result of systemic oppression. Finding words for what was felt but repressed, and therefore hard to articulate, consciousness-raising created a shared vocabulary and feminist ways of seeing. As Mitchell explains, it is a process of 'speaking the unspoken' and overlaps with 'serious psychoanalytic work'.[82] Women's Liberation was a movement built through collaborative acts of 'speaking the unspoken', and *Riddles* models how to listen for voices on this threshold.

In *Woman's Consciousness, Man's World* (1973), the feminist activist and historian Sheila Rowbotham writes eloquently about listening to silence and argues that we 'grasp' it in the 'moment in which it is breaking'.[83] This eruption of sound 'makes us understand what we could not hear before'.[84] In 1990, Rowbotham reflected on the National Women's Liberation Conference at Ruskin College in Oxford that she helped to organise. A fulcrum for feminist thought and activism, this event took place across three days in late February and early March of 1970. After twenty years, Rowbotham can still recall the excitement of seeing young women 'speaking with incredible passion at the microphone'.[85] In such scenes, people 'suddenly new to politics' were 'released' to 'express themselves'.[86]

In this broken silence, we can hear women resisting the idea that they are defined exclusively by motherhood. Along with equal pay, education and job opportunities, attendees of the Ruskin conference made free contraception, abortion on demand and 24-hour nurseries the focus of their activism. These demands cut through the idealisation of motherhood and made it clear maternal care is a form of work that requires infrastructure and equal compensation.

Riddles explores the histories restraining women from articulating such claims. Reflecting on her own struggle with such impediments, in 1989, Mulvey wrote about the writer's block she experienced after graduating from Oxford. The Women's Liberation Movement helped her work-through this 'long and painful struggle' with writing.[87] As she explains, 'suddenly a perspective on the world had unfolded that gave women a position to speak from', a way of seeing that challenged '[w]omen's exclusion from the *public* voice'.[88]

We can hear Mulvey taking up this position in 'The Spectacle is Vulnerable: Miss World, 1970'. Written with Margarita Jimenez, a fellow protestor, 'The Spectacle is Vulnerable' narrates the demonstration against the Miss World pageant that took place inside and outside the Royal Albert Hall. The essay was originally published anonymously in *Shrew*, the journal of the London Women's Liberation Workshop, an umbrella organisation that circulated writing and editing responsibilities among London's consciousness-raising groups. By staging this protest, Women's Liberation raised its voice before the whole world and questioned the conditions for women's visibility the beauty pageant displayed so blatantly. Continuing the protest through writing inscribed this feminist voice into history. Miss World, Mulvey and Jimenez argue, exemplifies what women are 'born to do': 'born to give birth, or if born pretty … to parade, silent and smiling'.[89] While the protestors were interrupting this spectacle with rattles, kazoos, whistles and shouts – 'Stop the cattle call!' – another protest was going on within the pageant. Black women were challenging the racial segregation of the British Empire. Jennifer Hosten from Grenada (who won the crown) and Pearl Jansen from South Africa (who was the runner-up) demonstrated that they were not 'born' to be excluded from the beauty associated with white femininity. This was a victory, though Jansen, as 'Miss Africa South', was made to pose for photographs with the white 'Miss South Africa' to create an image of unity designed to mollify Anti-Apartheid protests.

In *Riddles*, Louise also defies what she was 'born to do'. She refuses to give up the enclosed world she has created taking care of Anna, a refuge from the male gaze. The third shot depicts the consequences of this defiance in her marriage. Chris is leaving. As the intertitle explains, he 'cannot make her see reason / and get out more into the / world', though their split forces Louise out of the home. She moves into the public world of work as a single mother and translates the supposed irrationality of her desires into a collective feminist voice.

In the fourth shot, she walks hand-in-hand with Anna into a community daycare centre, filmed at the Holloway Neighbourhood Group on Lorraine Road. The undulating patterns of Ratledge's score have disappeared; the slippery alliterations of the Sphinx's poetry are also gone. They have been replaced by the voices of small children – the camera circles around the coloured tapestry of their crafts and activities – and the women who take care of them. Louise approaches Maxine, who wears a tangerine-orange blouse and a bright orange

silk headscarf. For the first time, we see Louise's face and it is synced to her voice. However, the loss of separating from Anna links them: 'Goodbye. Goodbye my love.' With a soothing voice, Maxine reassures Louise: 'Don't worry, we'll look after her.'

The fifth pan portrays Louise at a company switchboard, shot at a General Post Office training centre on Brompton Road. Before it begins, the intertitle attests to Louise's anxiety. In this narrow workspace, modestly dressed women sit close to each other on yellow office chairs. The pan begins by depicting the profiles of a few women, but as it circles the space we see the orderly row of their

backs turned. Facing the switchboards, they become an assembly line of women's voices. Echoing Louise and Maxine at the childcare centre, the musical lilts create a murmur of numbers, extensions and pleasantries – 'Would you like to hold the line, I'll try and find out what the extension is?' – that floats lyrically through the air. Woven into this soundscape are the clattering of plugs as the women skilfully connect and disconnect them from the switchboards' metal sockets. These sounds draw our attention to the fact that we are watching these women produce vocal commodities. Linked to the comforts transmitted by a pleasing image of a woman in film, the disembodied voices of the telephone operators are expected to have a gentle, soothing tone. They are 'acoustic mirrors' that validate the requests of the callers and direct their voices where they want to go. A scene of operators working creates an image that hums with the possibility of collective action.

When the camera gets to Louise, she is turned to the side of her switchboard to avoid the gaze of her supervisor. Louise whispers into her headset to make an outgoing call: 'Ah, Maxine. Good. Is Anna all right? Ah, that's a relief.' A telephone operator connects others, but Louise uses the switchboard to link her voice to Anna – and Maxine.

The rules Louise breaks by making an outside call have long histories. Replacing the boys originally slated for this work – they

proved to be too argumentative – the girls and young women who became switchboard operators in the late nineteenth century were subjected to heavy surveillance and terrible working conditions (forced to sit in place for long hours). Portrayed as superficial gossips in the visual media, their accents needed to sound middle class and from England (not from Ireland, Scotland, or Wales). Technically, any citizen of the British colonies could work as an operator, but racism kept women of colour from this lower-middle-class occupation.[90]

As the camera moves past Louise, she rushes to get off the phone and fumbles with the cords, frantically apologising to the person whose call she accidentally interrupted. The eye of the camera moves to a map of the globe pinned to the wall. An expansive counterpoint to the shadows of this crowded work area, the pale blue of the oceans echoes the images of Egypt in the film's earlier chapters. The flat neutrality of the map belies the exploitative reach of the British Empire that the decolonial cinemas of the 1960s and 1970s were beginning to reveal. Amid the operators, this image of the world asks us to think about the work women perform – whether as telephone operators, childcare workers or mothers – keeping people in touch across geographical distances inscribed by damaging histories.

The work of the operators points to the work that went into making *Riddles*. The sync sound of this shot asks us to imagine the

On set: Larry Sider, Laura Mulvey, Peter Wollen, Diane Tammes

challenges Sider faced behind the scenes. He had to follow the turn of
the camera enough to catch the women's voices but also stay out of
the frame. In a black-and-white photograph of the set, Sider is behind
the switchboard where a few women are sitting. He holds a portable
reel-to-reel analogue tape recorder, a Nagra, the industry standard at
the time, and stands across from Mulvey (wearing the blouse from
'Laura speaking'), Wollen and Tammes, who are gathered around
the camera. Sider used a shotgun microphone, which is capable
of picking up sounds from a distance (but it isn't visible in this
photograph). Like the operators, Sider is a skilled conduit of sound,
and by recording their performances, he becomes a figure for the
imaginary callers on the other side of the line.

The intertitle preceding the sixth shot is a Marxist-feminist
argument about mothers in capitalism. The operators bring the voice
into this argument. Mothers use their voices to mirror and care for
children, and while the telecommunication company utilises this skill,
it doesn't provide childcare. In the canteen where the operators take
their breaks, Louise starts a campaign to make this demand.

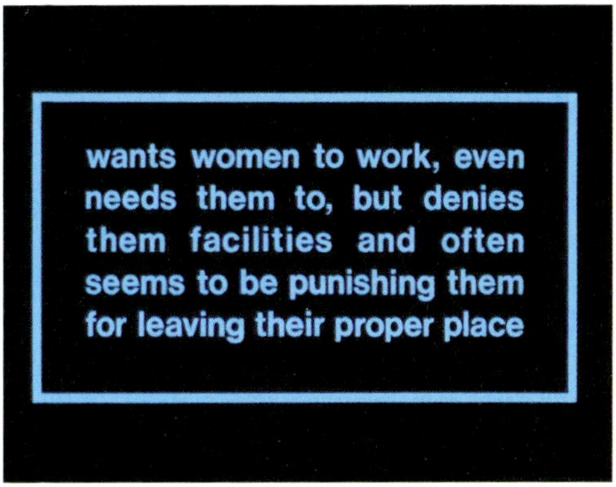

wants women to work, even
needs them to, but denies
them facilities and often
seems to be punishing them
for leaving their proper place

Through a door on the left, Louise enters the canteen with a
woman wearing a bright red skirt. Her gait is swift and confident. She
asks a woman standing in the kitchen for 'two teas' and she receives
her cup and saucer through the serving hatch. A woman in a pale blue
uniform and apron gathers the used dishes and puts them on a rolling
tray, which she pulls through the middle of the frame and back to the
kitchen. There are light clinking sounds as she creates a stack of cups
and saucers. Echoed by the operators stirring their tea with spoons,
these sounds were recorded during post-production and draw our
attention to another layer of work.

Louise walks out of the frame and stands near two women
sitting at a table. They begin a conversation about childcare. Many
of the extras in this scene worked at the BFI, and their dialogue was
improvised.[91] One woman, Lin, discusses a situation in which her
daughter Ellie became ill at the childminder's. She had to travel across
London to collect her, which increased her transportation costs.
The posters on the wall, all of which have to do with travel, inflect
this conversation with a cruel irony. Audible and assured, Louise
declares: 'There ought to be a nursery here, the company ought to
provide one.' Another woman smokes, drinks her tea and listens. The
burgundy sweater she wears rhymes with the TWA poster behind her.
She expresses a different point of view: 'I'm not sure. I don't really

like the idea of my kids here where I work. I like to think of work a
bit separate from the house.'

This is Claire Johnston. A media activist, film-maker, writer
and programmer who took her own life at the age of forty-seven,
Johnston was a member of the London Women's Film Group, a
collective that made documentary films such as *Betteshanger Kent*
(1972), *Women of the Rhondda* (1973) and *The Amazing Equal Pay
Show* (1974), which are devoted to working-class women's political
organising. She collaborated with women media workers in the UK,
lobbied the ACTT to listen to women's demands and played a key
role in the *Patterns of Discrimination* report. The text for which
Johnston is best known, 'Women's Cinema as Counter-Cinema'
(1973), is clearly in dialogue with Wollen's 'Godard and Counter-
Cinema' essay. It analyses how directors Dorothy Arzner and Ida
Lupino, women directors working in Hollywood during the 1920s
and 1930s, spoke from within the repressive language of dominant
cinematic conventions. At her conclusion, Johnston draws on
psychoanalysis to declare: 'In order to counter our objectification in
the cinema, our collective fantasies must be released: women's cinema
must embody the working through of desire.'[92]

To put this vision into motion, Johnston, Mulvey and Lynda
Myles curated the 'Women's Event' at the Edinburgh International

Film Festival in 1972. It was the first of its kind in Europe, and Myles was the first woman to run an international film festival. Over five days, they screened thirty-one films produced between 1923 and 1972.[93] Inspiring similar events around the globe, the 'Women's Event' was a public arena in which women screened their fantasies and worked-through their desires.

The scene at the canteen reminds us that childcare is necessary to sustain such projects and widen their impact. Sitting down at a table with another group of women, Louise expresses how much she hates leaving Anna. Carole, one of the women, describes her as the 'worrying type', but Louise refutes this by linking her anxieties to the difficulties of getting a child to the nursery: '[N]o wonder you're in a flap when you get here.' The camera circles the space and catches another group of women conversing about what they just heard. They question Louise's complaints and note that she hasn't worked at the company for long. But one woman, Mary, acknowledges that actually, Louise is right. The company should provide a nursery. Tammes's camera follows Louise's argument about employer-provided childcare as it circulates through the voices and minds of other women.

Riddles attests to the feeling, alive in the 1970s, that creating alternatives to capitalist exploitation was possible. Institutions such as the BFI, which Mulvey and Sue Clayton described as crucial

to the 'intellectual infrastructure of the radical film movement', supported that feeling.[94] In 1976, the BFI Production Board selected Mulvey and Wollen's grant application for *Riddles*, and they received £20,000 from the organisation. Mulvey and Wollen stipulated that everyone on set be paid the same, and for *Riddles*, this was £40 a week. According to Sider, this equal pay contributed to a rare sense of equality and collaboration on set.[95] No wonder so many of the people who contributed to *Riddles* – Maddox, Merrison, Ratledge, Sider, Tammes – would work with Mulvey and Wollen on subsequent films.

In the mid-1970s, under the leadership of Peter Sainsbury, the BFI Production Board became responsive to the radical film movement and dispersed more money to independent productions. Sainsbury, a founding editor of *Afterimage*, encouraged Mulvey and Wollen to apply for a grant. Two film-making collectives attentive to gender and class also received funding during this period: the London Women's Film Group, for *Whose Choice?* (1976) and *Rapunzel, Let Down Your Hair* (1978), and the Berwick Street Film Collective, for *Nightcleaners*.

The funding Mulvey and Wollen received from the BFI was one significant part of their relationship to this institution founded in 1933 to 'encourage the art of film'. Wollen worked in the Education Department at the BFI under the generous auspices of Paddy Whannel. From the Scottish working class, Whannel ran the department from 1957 to 1971 and hired Wollen in 1966, his 'first proper job'.[96] In 1967, he gave Wollen the responsibility for organising seminars devoted to emerging work in film studies, which helped the BFI become a centre for film theory.

Hollywood became a bond between them, as Whannel was devoted to popular commercial cinema. This investment gave rise to his collaboration with Stuart Hall, the Jamaican-British intellectual who would become a defender of and interlocuter for Black British film-makers who formed collectives in the 1980s in response to systemic racism. Hall and Whannel's co-authored book, *The Popular Arts* (1964), foresaw the fields of cultural and media studies.[97] Whannel's attention to commercial cinema put him at odds with the

BFI's mission to foster British film culture and stave off Hollywood's influence. And yet, Wollen considered Whannel's tenure at the BFI a 'turning point for the development of film studies in Britain'.[98]

In the 1970s, women were trying to access and create similar structures of authority and influence. Assumptions women internalised about their own passivity made this difficult. The next pan – the seventh of the thirteen – composes a picture of urban travel to portray women working-through those impediments. It depicts Louise, Maxine and two other women in a yellow van moving through a roundabout at the junction of Carlton Vale and Kilburn Park Road. Patsy Nightingale (a producer) drives the van and Rosalind Delmar (a feminist writer, editor and activist) plays the role of a trade unionist. The conversation about childcare Louise started at the canteen has become a campaign and the travel posters have been replaced by actual transportation. The four women are on their way to a meeting Maxine has arranged to find out whether the union will support their demands.

It is a cloudy grey day in London. The shot begins by portraying an urban landscape: a footbridge that goes over the roundabout; the brick buildings behind it; chain-link fences; power lines; and the central island with its dried yellow grass and sparse greenery blowing in the wind. The humble scene evokes Italian neorealism

and its focus on the facts and contingencies of actual places. There is a stationary yellow van parked at the far end of the frame and we soon see that this is the van in which the women will be travelling. We can't see them, but we hear them talking. They are waiting for a little boy (played by Chad Wollen, Mulvey and Wollen's son) who will come across the footbridge. Maxine will hand him something – we don't know what – to give to his mother. This exchange brings the unpredictable textures of everyday realities to the scene and connects it to children.

A few seconds before the little boy arrives, the camera starts moving at a different pace and the van is no longer in the frame. We hear the engine start and the clicks of the turn signal. The sounds of the women's voices begin connecting up with the image of the car on screen. Eventually, Louise can be discerned through the window in the back seat – a moving portrait in profile.

Composing a circle within a circle, the shot at the roundabout demonstrates the technical skills and endurance of Tammes and Sider. Assisted by Jane Jackson, Tammes was in the back of a Mini-Moke (a front-wheel-drive utility convertible) driven around the roundabout, and Sider was crouched down in the car below the windows recording the women's voices. Wollen, who is also in the Mini-Moke, devised this intricate shot and was precisely realising it with a stopwatch.

Executing the shot at the roundabout: Diane Tammes, Jane Jackson and Peter Wollen

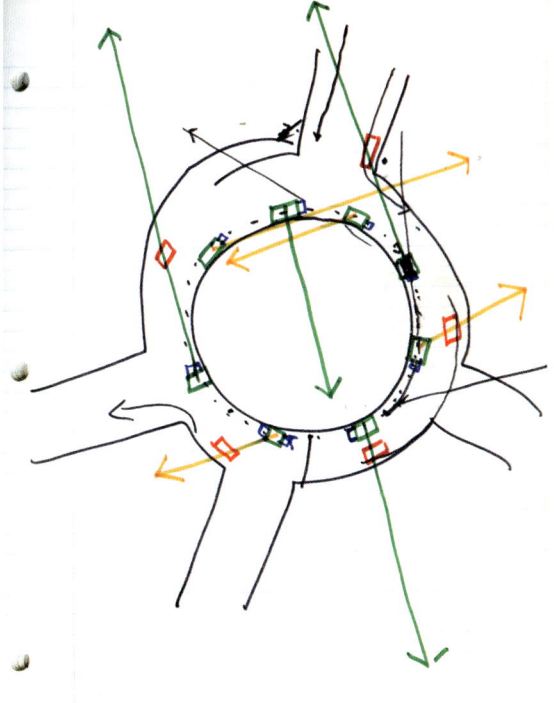

Peter Wollen's drawing for the seventh 360-degree panning shot in Chapter 4, 'Louise's story told in thirteen shots': the roundabout with vehicle and camera movement, c. 1977 (© Laura Mulvey)

Together they were inscribing a claim to a collective feminist voice into the history of cinema and revealing its complexity. A 360-degree pan is disorienting enough, but doubling it makes it more so. Serpentine and convoluted, the two pans connect to the difficult questions the women pose about childcare in the workplace. Because there are so few models to draw on, they do not arrive at definitive answers.

The seventh shot is a feminist argument about movement. With a car (in this case, a van), you can act on your desires to move, go and do. Reflecting on the impact the Ruskin conference had on her, the feminist historian Sally Alexander attests to the restraints she felt as a young woman. The car, and its association with freedom and mobility, is a figure for the actions men were permitted. As she explains,

Men did things. Unlike women. They went out, and they took taxis across London, they travelled, they wrote plays. They thought, 'Let's go on holiday', and they got into cars and drove off. I wanted to do things. I really did. I also wanted to have children, and be married.[99]

Linked to writing, her desire for mobility clashed with the desire to marry and have children. The image of the van at the roundabout brings the desire to move and motherhood together.

Where does the idea that women cannot – or should not – 'get in a car and dr[ive] off' come from? Why do the capacity and desire to have children become limitations? Why is the freedom of movement aligned with masculinity? In the early 1970s, Mulvey became a member of a reading group that brought psychoanalysis to bear on questions like these. Mitchell, Delmar and Alexander were members of this group, so was the artist Mary Kelly and the film critic and broadcaster Margaret Walters. Together they read the work of Freud and Lacan and placed it in dialogue with thinkers such as Claude Lévi-Strauss, Karl Marx and Friedrich Engels. The concept of the unconscious accounted for the patriarchal blind spots in this work and offered glimpses into the psychic dimensions of women's oppression – long, shadowy histories that needed to be excavated and worked-through. Psychoanalysis gave them a vocabulary for describing both the stubborn hold of patriarchal culture and the psychic mechanisms that coerce women into internalising restraints so they feel the freedom to 'drive off' is not theirs.

The extraordinary work that emerged from this reading group attests to the energy unleashed when women come together to read and listen to the sounds of the longest revolution. The next shot, which takes place in a shopping mall – the Arndale Centre on Wandsworth High Street – raises questions about capitalist saturation and the challenges it poses to resistant collectivities. The colours of the neon signs – cobalt blue, cherry red, lemon yellow – are seductive, and for the soundtrack, Ratledge created a slow, consistent wave of soothing sounds. All of the shops illustrate consumer culture's long appeal to women, catering to the care they are expected to give (grocery store, pharmacy) and the images they are expected to create (clothing, jewellery, interior decoration). Louise and Maxine move through the mall with Anna in a pushchair, but they appear a minute after the pan has begun. Placed at the far end of this long shot and woven among the other shoppers, this feminist friendship is hard to see in the context of the mall and the hyper-capitalism it symbolises.

The textual fragment that begins the ninth shot indicates Louise was fired from her job. The first word is 'mistakes', and it starts to

mistakes, so the Union won't take up her case. Although she hopes to keep the campaign going from outside, she can't help worrying about

bring the collective voice of feminism, to which Louise attached her desires, into crisis. This shot was filmed at Barham Park, a playground at the junction of Harrow High Road and Bridgewater Road. At the beginning of the pan, we see an infant in a blue pram and a white woman helping a little girl as she tries to climb a jungle gym ladder. This little girl has blonde hair and wears a tangerine coat with fluffy white trim, lavender trousers and red shoes. The ladder is connected to a large lime-green metal circle, a figure for the eye of the camera and the pan's circular framing. All around them is the deep green of the grass and the trees, which creates a thick background for the subtle details of the *mise en scène* to come into the foreground.

The little girl in the tangerine coat is Georgia, the daughter of Dinah Stabb, the actor who plays Louise. The woman attending to her is Christine Smith, the childminder on the set. Since Stabb had Georgia, Mulvey and Wollen needed someone to watch her, and they paid Smith the same flat rate as the actors and the technicians. Childcare is central to Louise's story, and the directors extend it to include the conditions on the set and the lives of people who worked on it.

Accompanied by Ratledge's score, the voice of the Sphinx returns, but with a difference. The sound of her voice remains the same, but she now speaks in the language of feminist theory and explores the kinds of thinking feminism makes possible. Evoking the circular form of the pans and the simple nursery-rhyme patterns of the music, the Sphinx states: 'Questions arose which seemed to form a linked ring, each raising the next until they led the argument back to its original point of departure.' In the distance, at the edge of the park, the camera passes over Louise. Wearing a sweater with wide green stripes, she is sitting on a wooden bench and reading a magazine. Anna stands and Louise holds her at the waist. Then another woman comes into view: she is propping up a little girl who sits at the front of a blue rocking horse with an elongated body.

The child's rocking creates a visual rhythm, a counterpoint to the slower pace of the music and the reflections of the Sphinx. Louise then crosses the frame holding Anna's hand and passes by the woman holding the little girl upright on the blue horse. This is Rosamund Howe, Mulvey's sister, and Natalie, her niece.

The voice of the Sphinx begins posing questions about women, work, childcare, domestic labour, motherhood and oppression. In what could be a transcript of the reading group Mulvey participated in, and, more broadly, the shift in Women's Liberation from political activism to feminist theory, the Sphinx asks,

How does women's struggle relate to class struggle? Is patriarchy the main enemy for women? Does the oppression of women work on the unconscious as well as the conscious? What would the politics of the unconscious be like? How necessary is being-a-mother to women, in reality or imagination?

Drawing on feminism, Marxism and psychoanalysis, these questions highlight the interrelated issues that are at stake in Louise's life as a single mother.

Louise does not speak in this scene, but she is reading *Spare Rib*, the most iconic of the feminist publications to come out of the Women's Liberation Movement in Britain. Like *Women Speaking*, *Red Rag*, *Shrew* and *Trouble & Strife*, *Spare Rib* put a collective feminist voice into print and became a forum for women to be heard. Mulvey published a number of articles on film and visual culture in the magazine. Focused on consciousness-raising, activism and the politics of everyday life, *Spare Rib* was a straightforward address to women, which is why Mulvey and Wollen chose it for Louise, an unpretentious character in the midst of figuring out what feminism means to her.[100] Now distanced from the campaign for childcare in the workplace, reading *Spare Rib* links her to its feminist aspirations.

The wide green space of the playground allowed Mulvey and Wollen to place mothers and women taking care of children in relationship to each other. As Louise guides Anna to the wooden

swings and Anna places her scruffy teddy bear in one of them, the camera circles back to the childminder pushing the pram away from the playground structures. Smith holds out her hand to encourage little Georgia, reluctant to leave the playground, to come along. The pan captures the slow meandering of children and the patience their care requires.

Louise and Anna are once again in the frame. They approach a slide and pause as though deciding whether Anna can safely go down it. They move to the ladder and the pan circles back to the first image in which the childminder held Georgia as she tentatively moved up and down the steps. This time, the little girl is Anna, and Louise stands to the side, reading *Spare Rib* and holding Anna's teddy bear. (They are both objects of comfort.) This rhyming of positions highlights the connections among the women in the scene, but the wide expanse of the park also evokes their isolation. Strangers in an urban playground might sense or see each other, but they rotate through the space alone. The children are young – the large geometric shapes of the climbing frames highlight how small they are – and they need to be closely held and watched. Each caretaking set becomes a tiny world.

The movement of Louise and Anna around the playground seems haphazard. The intertitle preceding the shot mentions 'worry' and Louise looks distressed. Speaking through feminism's collective voice has become even more complex. After asking, '[a]re campaigns for child-care a priority for women now?', which links to Louise's efforts to insist on company-provided childcare, the Sphinx concludes her reflections:

Question after question arose, revolving in her mind without reaching any clear conclusion. They led both out into society and back into her own memory. Future and past seemed to be locked together. She felt a gathering of strength but no certainty of success.

An example of psychoanalytic thinking, this passage tracks the movement of Louise's mind. It shows how she is puzzling through her thoughts and the situation in which she finds herself. The music contributes to the movement between the interior and the exterior. Composed of sombre three-note melodies slowly layered on top of each other, Ratledge creates small circles of sound and stitches them into the camera's wider turns mapping the edges of the playground. Both resonate with the looped movement of Louise's thoughts, as they go 'out into society' but also 'back into her own memory'.

Layered with the movement of feminist thought, the scene at the park creates a complicated path for Louise to continue participating in the outside world and speaking in feminism's collective voice. It also creates another space – inflected by, but separate from, feminist collectivities – where her own voice can reside. Mulvey argues that in addition to screening collective fantasies and working-through desires, feminist avant-garde film-makers in the 1970s were looking for ways to 'find a voice for women's interiority, for the inside of the mind itself, as well as for its silences'.[101] The concluding shots portray Louise turning back to her own life to find this space for her interior voice. This is not a move away from feminism or its political insistence on equality. Instead, it is an exploration of what feminism makes possible at the level of the unconscious.

5 Listening for Fantasies

While *Riddles* guides us towards the subtle modes of looking, reading and listening feminism requires, the film reaches beyond claims to equality and into desire. Mulvey and Wollen fostered these modes of response by portraying the connection between Louise and Women's Liberation in panoramic slices of time that do not fit together into a cohesive story of progress. The film composes a feminist voice that slowly emerges from the private, moves into the public and then circles back to the private again, collapsing their distinctions. Along this circuitous route, *Riddles* touches upon other histories of exploitation that are entwined with feminism's utopic desires.

In the tenth shot of 'Louise's story', Louise 'br[ings] herself back into her past', as the intertitle explains, and visits her mother (Peter Wollen's mother, Winifred Wollen) with Maxine and Anna. In an enclosed urban garden, the directors continue writing the film's language of sensual pleasure. Holding and looking at photographs together, Louise and Maxine bring touch to the image. With a playful, loving voice, the grandmother speaks to Anna about watering the tomato plants so they are a 'lovely and blazing' red, deepening the film's engagement with colour. The shot comes to a close with Louise, framed by green foliage, apples and flowers, watching her mother care for her daughter. While letting Anna go, she is also reinforcing the value of the maternal line. She turns back to sit with Maxine and continue looking at photographs.

This scene raises questions about the role of Maxine in the film. This character, played by a Black actor, stands apart from the image of family history created for Louise. Since reproduction is bound to our understanding of race, and the maternal line has often been figured as the origin of racial difference, the portrayal of three generations of white women brings Maxine's Blackness into relief.[102]

In one respect, it seems right that Maxine is not made to represent Blackness or racial oppression. She is simply part of the multi-racial metropolis in which *Riddles* takes place. At the same time, the film does not gesture to the racial inequalities of late twentieth-century London. Though Jordine, the actor who plays Maxine, was born in Jamaica, Britain's presence in the Caribbean does not inflect the story, and the afterlives of imperialism are not actively placed in the present tense of the film but evoked through the mythical terrain of ancient Egypt. Created by the whiteness projected onto the image of Britain, these absences seem to hover around the film unconsciously and asked to be worked-through.

The truncated portrayal of Maxine has been criticised. Writing in *Screen* in the late 1980s, Isaac Julien and Kobena Mercer situate *Riddles* in a set of avant-garde films that rely upon the 'romanticist image-reservoir' in which 'blackness is valorised as emblematic of outsiderness and oppositionality'.[103] There is truth to this assessment, but it can be placed alongside Julien's discussion of the generative effect of Mulvey's work on his own. For the Sankofa Film and Video Collective, a group of Black independent film-makers of which Julien was a founding member, Mulvey's psychoanalytic understanding of the cinematic image was a revolutionary opening. Sankofa came together in the early 1980s to make films about interrelated forms of racial violence – police brutality and fixed images of Blackness that occluded the flux and contestation of identity in the Black diaspora.[104] As Hall pointed out, these film-makers were attempting to 'find a new language', and Julien shows they were, following Mulvey, writing a 'new language of desire'.[105]

For Julien, Mulvey's work 'raised the question of the desire of the viewer, and its relation to the desired self and desiring bodies on screen'.[106] In *Looking for Langston* (1989), a poetic essay film devoted to the fantasies of queer Black culture in the 1980s (and the attendant issues of AIDS and the rise of neoconservatism), Julien worked with the gaze as a structure that 'imbue[s]' the act of looking with a 'sense of erotic desire' that interweaves identity with the poetics of identification.[107] To 'imbue' images of men with the complications of that eroticism, he decided to work closely with Nina Kellgren, a female cinematographer who began working in film because she was hired by none other than Tammes.

The eleventh shot of 'Louise's story' continues to suggest the complexity of Maxine's role in *Riddles*. It takes place in Chris's studio. To signal a turn into the past, the pan starts moving counterclockwise. At mid-range, the camera portrays Maxine showing Louise how to create an optical trick with a mirror and a Camel cigarette packet. Instead of reversing the writing on the packet, the cellophane puts it, as Maxine explains, 'right way round'. A reflection on the distortions of mirrors and images, this part of the shot is about learning to read the commodity, in this case a packet of cigarettes decorated with an image of Egypt that covers over histories of slave labour. (We don't see the packet, but Louise refers to its iconic camel.) This scene of Louise and Maxine reading the cigarette pack is an example of the problematic trope of the Black character with powers of insight helping the white protagonist at the centre of a film. However, by portraying the act of reading, it also represents the desire to work-through histories of exploitation and create a feminist perspective equally attentive to the hierarchies of gender, race and class.

Chris is attempting to be part of this process. In a studio filled with editing equipment, silver film reels and strips of 16mm film, he has been making a documentary about a woman artist. The artist is Mary Kelly, Mulvey and Wollen's friend and collaborator. The project is *Post-Partum Document* (1973–9), an installation that rewrites conceptual art's sober displays of information to portray the mother's language, desires and losses. In this film within a film, Chris contributes to writing a new language of desire, though his voice is, as Wollen acerbically puts it, 'redolent of the goodwill and sound sense of patriarchy in its full banality'.[108]

Before Chris shows his footage, Louise solidifies their separation by telling him she wants to sell their home and live with Maxine. Chris smokes and absorbs this announcement with irritated resignation. Asserting his knowledge of the market, a vestige of white patriarchal masculinity's link to property ownership, he remarks that it isn't a good time to sell. Without hesitation, Louise asserts: 'It's a good time for me to sell.' She is detaching herself from the image of the obedient wife who aligns her voice with that of her husband's. Allowing her desires to move across the lines of racial difference is part of that detachment.

As Mayer observes, the scene in Chris's studio brings the 'oppositional gaze' into *Riddles*.[109] The 'oppositional gaze' is hooks's term for the critical reading skills Black women have developed to engage with visual worlds that 'construct [their] presence as absence'.[110] Since racism and sexism are written into vision and visual culture, hooks argues that Black women know how to look critically at images and identify their deceptive appeals. Discussing the fact that feminist film theory mostly ignored issues of race in the 1970s and early 1980s, hooks cites Mulvey's reflections on feminism puncturing her love of Hollywood cinema and states: 'Mulvey arrived at that location of disaffection that is the starting point for many black women approaching cinema within the lived harsh reality of racism.'[111] The image of Louise and Maxine playing with the Camel packet illustrates hooks's point. Maxine already knows how to circumvent the distortions of the mirror and shows Louise how to see images of writing differently. Together these characters are reading against the neutral grain of whiteness embedded in the visual concept of 'woman', which erases, hooks argues, historical differences among women.[112] This challenge to the whiteness of 'woman' does not seem to be a conscious part of the film-makers' intentions, but *Riddles* shows us that feminism is more than a conscious political project. It has an unconscious that is full of transformative potential, not just blind spots and conservative limitations.

The twelfth and penultimate shot of 'Louise's story' takes place in Maxine's apartment. The cryptic intertitle alludes to Mulvey's 'Visual Pleasure' and makes the imaginative world of their friendship as a refuge from the imperative to perform as images for others.

Mulvey and Wollen filmed this shot in the upstairs studio of the avant-garde film-maker Stephen Dwoskin, a founding member of the London Film-makers' Co-op who lived across the street at 208 Ladbroke Grove.[113] The walls and windows of Dwoskin's studio, where he composed his own subversive meditations on the gaze, are decorated with red curtains. Saturated in red, this scene is a return to the domestic interior, but the pleasures of maternal care have transformed into an erotic, interracial and potentially queer collaboration. It reflects the collaborations that emerged from

as in dreams, but takes the form of masquerade, locked into a world of images where each needs to feel sheltered within another's gaze to find

Women's Liberation and shows feminism beginning to move, like Tammes's pan, horizontally, circumventing the vertical hierarchies of patriarchal imperialism.

In this shot, we first see Louise through an oval mirror. Reading a book at a dressing table, she wears a navy-blue robe decorated with white flowers. Draped behind her are the thick red curtains, and the fuchsia blouse Mulvey wore in 'Laura speaking' has been placed over the back of the chair on which she sits. This sartorial citation from the second chapter connects director and protagonist and further inscribes the visual language Mulvey and Wollen have composed with the colours, patterns and textures of clothing.

Across the room, we see Maxine. She wears an orange silk robe and applies make-up to her face with glamorous flourishes, as if she is creating a sculpture. Her image appears in a dressing-room mirror framed with large circular lights. This mirror evokes the work of preparation before going on set and links to Jordine's career in theatre, film and television. However, this moving portrait of Maxine is not about perfecting an image of prettiness for visual consumption, but the sensuous, erotic pleasure of crafting an image of oneself in the eyes of another woman.

This shot composes a different way of understanding femininity. The mirrors, make-up, colourful fabric and beautiful clothing are

materials for imaginative self-fashioning, not for catering to the male gaze. By arranging images of Louise and Maxine so they are layered in relationship to each other, this scene models ways of witnessing how rich women's fantasies are when they don't capitulate to masculinist desires. Furthermore, within this visual splendour, feminine beauty is not exclusiveness to whiteness, and Mulvey and Wollen have imbued the decorative (often associated with racial difference) with value and depth.

The camera circles the room to the calm and magisterial sounds of Ratledge's score and lovingly reveals a tapestry of decorative

objects – mirrors, frames, plants, sculptures, paintings, quilts – with richly textured surfaces. Many of these objects were borrowed from the directors' friends and family.[114] The pan also pays homage to the *mise en scène* of melodrama, its precise staging of objects and its deliberate layering of cinematic techniques.[115] Mulvey has a long-standing interest in melodrama and its anxious focus on the sexuality of mothers, and she wrote about melodrama in *Spare Rib* to stress its significance for Women's Liberation. She argues that the genre creates a visual language that indirectly attests to the suppression of women's voices.[116]

These debts to melodrama show that *Riddles* is not a complete rejection of Hollywood (as if that were really possible). Instead, it is a subtle attempt to expand the slim openings Hollywood gave women to imagine their relationships to each other. In her reading of Douglas Sirk's *Imitation of Life* (1959), Mulvey tracks how the film quietly strains against rigid definitions of white femininity, motherhood, racial difference and labour within US capitalism.[117] This constellation of issues is pertinent to the friendship between Louise and Maxine, and the film's citation of melodrama's themes suggests that the dilemmas of motherhood cannot be solved if women of colour are not in the frame.

As the camera moves across Maxine's image, Louise asks about the text she is reading – 'What does it mean?' – and we learn she is

reading from a book of Maxine's writing. An intimate conversation about childhood memories, dreams, fairy tales and fantasy unfolds and becomes part of the music. Louise reads another long passage, full of mythical resonances and the rich sensuality of fabric – '[W]hen I looked at the sea, it seemed to be made of silk' – and Maxine listens intently to her own words in her friend's voice. Resembling the one-on-one encounter of psychoanalysis, together they are listening for the fantasies that can arise when women are free to see and hear themselves outside the demand to mirror others. Ratledge's music, with its simple pattern of low, heavy sounds decorated with shimmering vibrations, contributes to the shot's intricate screen of materials and the deep listening it models. The future the music imagines is haunted by loss. Jordine was married to Denys Irving, the man who designed the multi-track synthesisers upon which Ratledge composed the score. Irving died in a hang-gliding accident in August 1976.

As Louise poses another question about Maxine's writing – 'What does that mean I wonder' – we see the reflection of Tammes in a mirror, carefully turning the mobile head on which the camera is mounted. This reflection announces her significance as the cinematographer. She is the woman with the skills to make this feminist avant-garde film possible. As the camera moves across this historic opening to rewrite the patriarchal masculinity behind the

scenes, Maxine responds to Louise's question about her text: 'I don't know exactly. That's why I wrote it. I hoped I would understand it more.' Maxine's exploratory writing, Louise's curious reading, Tammes's moving camera – together they create a layered image of feminist collectivity that holds together sameness and difference, knowing and unknowing.

The last shot in 'Louise's story' portrays Louise and Anna walking through the Egyptian galleries of the British Museum. A testament to imperial dominance, the British Museum returns the film to its Egyptian themes and, as it states in the intertitle, links them to the 'power of a different language'. After the extended rewriting of white women's visibility across 'Louise's story', the scene connects the feminist defiance of patriarchal authority to decolonising the image of Egypt as a 'dark continent' that has justified thefts of culture, labour and land. Over the images of mummies (pun intended) decorated with hieroglyphs and encased in glass, the Sphinx tells a poetic story of generational transmission. It suggests that in the future, Anna could realise the feminist and anti-racist possibilities evoked by her mother's relationship with Maxine.

When the last pan concludes, 'Louise's story' abruptly ends. There is no indication of where Louise will go or what she will do. This rejection of closure reminds us that she is a character composed for and made visible within the fictional world of *Riddles*. The chapters that follow attest to the transformations that become possible when we see images of women engaged in the project of listening for fantasies in women's voices – including their own.

In 'Acrobats', the chapter that comes immediately after 'Louise's story', gymnasts and circus performers juggle, climb and swing from ropes. With their limber, agile bodies, they do handstands, cartwheels and backbends. 'Acrobats' recalls Eisenstein's use of circus and music-hall attractions in the theatrical performances that prefigured his work as a film-maker. And to complement the images of women rewriting assumptions they are passive and inert, Ratledge created a percussive piece of music with sonorous beats overlaid with high, bubbly notes that sound as though they come from a xylophone. Celebrating images of women that are elastic and vital, 'Acrobats' visualises a poetics of the body's capacity to defy gravity and the pull of patriarchal history. These expressions of movement evoke the possibilities of play before girls confront the limited ways the world so often perceives them. It also draws from Mulvey's own childhood memories of practising gymnastics with her sister.[118]

The images placed at the beginning and end of 'Acrobats' were shot in black and white. Performing in front of curtains, the bodies of the acrobats are doubled by shadows and create pictographs in the air. Like the refilmed imagery of 'Stones', the shots in the middle were reprinted, but in bright candy colours that recall the neon signs at the shopping mall: lemon yellow, emerald green, turquoise and cobalt blue, tangerine orange, fuchsia pink. In a few of the images, depictions of the gymnasts have been superimposed on another, which suggests the collectivity of their performance. Sider recalls the challenge he and Carola Klein faced when combining the filmed movements in the editing process. They drew silhouettes of the acrobats on blue celluloid to overlay one image over another and then map the dissolves. For him, this process embodied the 'handmade', 'arts and crafts' quality of film-making Mulvey and Wollen loved.[119]

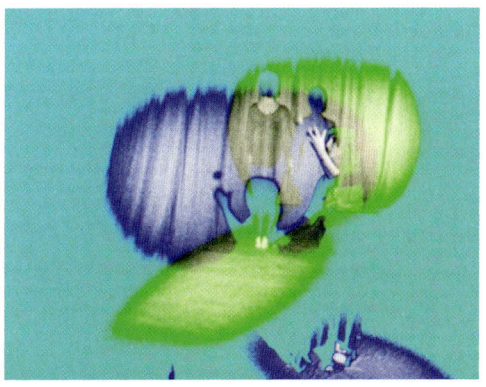

'Laura listening', the next chapter of *Riddles*, is the counterpoint to 'Laura speaking'. It revisits the image of Mulvey at her desk. She is no longer addressing her audience about the Sphinx, but listening to a recording of her voice. Playing the tape, she hears herself discuss Karl Marx's concept of the commodity fetish as described in the first volume of *Capital*: '"… into the social hieroglyphic. Later on, we try to decipher the hieroglyphic, to get behind the secret …"' Wearing glasses, she writes her words down and presses the buttons of the recorder with a sense of urgency, even frustration. It is crucial to inscribe this material into history.

Wollen identifies the stakes of the scene: 'As she listens, Laura writes: her inscription is a function of the voice to which she is listening.'[120] The citation from Marx is an aspect of the lecture we did not hear earlier, though the hieroglyph, a figure for the 'commodity fetish' that covers over the forces of exploitation that often rely on the hierarchies of race and gender, returns the film to its Egyptian themes. A scene of retrospective reading and a claim to women's work, 'Laura listening' takes us back to the switchboard operators creating commodities with their voices and Louise and Maxine reversing the image of writing on the cigarette packet. The chapter tells us *Riddles* is not a complete picture of feminism. Instead, it stages a process of reflection and return, a working-through of historical gaps.

The last chapter, 'Puzzle ending', depicts a mercury puzzle. It is made of plastic and alludes to the labyrinths built under the Egyptian pyramids. The shiny glow of the mercury ball contrasts with the toy's texture, which gives it a handmade feel, and it is Mulvey's hands navigating the puzzle. An image of the film, the puzzle materialises the challenge posed to feminist thinking by the language of patriarchal culture. However, by watching the two glowing balls of mercury slip through the narrow spaces of this miniature labyrinth, viewers are invited to reflect on feminism as a fluid, revolutionary 'movement' in which the present and the past, the conscious and

the unconscious, seeing and listening are always but unpredictably touching each other.

If read this way, the puzzle becomes a dream image of feminism circling back to its pasts and moving into its futures simultaneously. It challenges the demand for feminism to appear in ordered blocks of linear time and create a clear image of its progress. Mulvey solves the puzzle: the mercury arrives at the centre. She also disperses the mercury by shaking it, ending *Riddles* with an image that is open-ended, suspended in shiny threads of uncertainty.

Conclusion: Continued by You

I cannot remember the first time I saw *Riddles*, but I still hold
the strange mixture of pleasure and discomfort that arose from
my initial encounter with the film, the odd sense that it was both
foreign and familiar. I wrote about *Riddles* in my first book, and as I
searched for the words to describe its poetic undoing of the cinematic
image, I thought about my mother. She introduced me to feminism
through her own embrace of a vague but significant idea – instead
of remaining faithful housewives in unhappy marriages, women
could shape their lives with their own desires. Paperback books
and popular films expressed this possibility and became part of my
mother's life, filtering down to me.

  I vividly remember my mother's copy of *The Women's Room*
(1977) by Marilyn French. Upon the paperback's bright yellow
cover, the word 'Women's' was scrawled in thick black pen over the
carefully printed red letters that spelled out 'The Ladies' Room'. (At
the time, I was curious about the sex parts.) The layers of writing
on the cover of this feminist bestseller connected to the doodles my
mother absent-mindedly drew on receipts and bits of paper that
were placed on top of the bulky telephone book that sat on the
kitchen counter. I can still see the traces of my mother's handwriting
imprinted on the waxy yellow cover. Attesting to the pleasures
and anxieties of claiming a certain form of freedom, those traces
introduced the idea that women's words and fantasies mattered.
Perhaps because I first encountered feminism in this way, at its
edges – through books I stole and doodles I tried to decipher – now as
a scholar I am more interested in feminism as it manifests cryptically
in aesthetic objects such as *Riddles*.

  With its kaleidoscopic arrangements of images, texts and
sounds, *Riddles* tunes our senses to the longest revolution and its

challenge to the stubbornly entrenched assumption that women naturally mirror others. The film's chorus of voices is key to this challenge. Individual and collective, private and public, within the film's narrative and outside of it, attached to images and free from them, the voices of women in *Riddles* disassembles fixed definitions of both women and feminism.

Committed to complexity, Mulvey and Wollen encourage viewers to take the liberal insistence on women's equality further, and, as Jacqueline Rose puts it, 'burrow beneath its surface to confront the subterranean aspects of history and the human mind'.[121] By yoking psychoanalytic concepts to the tropes of avant-garde cinema, *Riddles* models the 'burrowing' for which Rose calls and invites us to return to the utopian aspirations of the 1970s as imaginative resources for confronting what Mulvey calls the 'psyche's political reality' in the twenty-first century.[122]

The film's address to viewers makes *Riddles* a lot more than a historical artifact. It asks us to continue working-through unconscious investments in women's silence. It gives us a rich set of tools for reflecting on the renewed suppression of women's voices – I am thinking of the limits placed on reproductive justice in the US – while also registering feminism's substantial and long-term impact. The popularity of the 'male gaze' is a sign of this impact, and so is the array of literary and visual artwork that renders experiences of motherhood in all their historical and psychic complexity.

The intricacy of Mulvey and Wollen's film both contrasts and contests a simple but consequential fantasy circulating through social media that images of women's bodies are always there for the taking. This fantasy is intimately connected to the rise of authoritarian leaders who tap into long histories of patriarchal power and rely on a one-dimensional concept of 'woman' as defined by her reproductive capacities and assigned the work of reproducing (both symbolically and biologically) the fictions of racial purity and the imaginary cohesion of nations. *Riddles* stages a process in which these fantasies start to come undone. As we saw in the portrayal of Louise and

Maxine in the room with mirrors, it contributes to detaching feminism's public voice from images of whiteness and, by composing a scene in which viewers are listening to the fantasies written by women of colour, poses a question – what could women become if patriarchal masculinity was not so heavily defended?

The film's resistance to closure suggests that Mulvey and Wollen hoped future viewers would become collaborators in the process of posing this question. Reflecting on their commitment to making open-ended films, Mulvey recalls that they were struck by the Brechtian conclusion of Samuel Fuller's *Run of the Arrow* (1957). At the end of this Technicolor Western, the title states: "'The end of this story will be written by you.'"[123] This piece of cinematic writing addresses viewers directly and asks them to link the film to their present tense. Singular and plural, the second-person pronoun 'you' is open to every viewer. *Riddles* does not tell viewers to 'finish' the film or the history from which it emerged. It asks them to continue writing the connections between feminism and the unconscious, a pursuit that makes it harder to see progress but also gets closer to the deep transformation the world needs.

Sometimes when I reflect on my engagement with *Riddles*, I think of Mulvey and Wollen's film listening to me. It has helped me create a space in which I can write and work-through the narrow destinies women have been granted. To write, I have to quieten the voices that mute my own and pull me into thinking I should give myself over to the needs and desires of others. At the same time, *Riddles* encourages me to envision a more just world in which the care mothers freely give is not exclusively attached to women and can become a valued aesthetic and political project. *Riddles* opens spaces for discovering voices inside the mind, voices capable of moving through the puzzles patriarchal definitions of care have placed before women, and along the way, writing a new language of desire.

Notes

1 Griselda Pollock and Laura Mulvey, 'Laura Mulvey in Conversation with Griselda Pollock', *Studies in the Maternal* 2, no. 1 (2010), pp. 1–13 (p. 7). Available at: <https://doi.org/10.16995/sim.101> (accessed August 2024).

2 Conversation with Laura Mulvey, June 2023.

3 Peter Wollen, 'Godard and Counter-Cinema: *Vent d'Est*', in *Readings and Writings: Semiotic Counter-Strategies* (London: Verso, 1982 [1972]), pp. 79–91.

4 Laura Mulvey, Unpublished Manuscript. Laura Mulvey, *Afterimages: On Cinema, Women and Changing Times* (London: Reaktion Books, 2019).

5 Peter Wollen, 'An Alphabet of Cinema', in *Paris Hollywood: Writings on Film* (London and New York: Verso Books, 2002 [2001]), pp. 1–21 (p. 3).

6 Ibid., pp. 4, 5.

7 Laura Mulvey, 'Americanitis: European Intellectuals and Hollywood Melodrama', in *Fetishism and Curiosity: Cinema and the Mind's Eye* (London: BFI/Palgrave, 2013 [1996]), pp. 19–33 (p. 20).

8 Simon Hammond, 'Knight's Moves', *New Left Review* 124 (July/August 2020), pp. 5–40 (p. 6).

9 Laura Mulvey and Peter Wollen, 'From Cinephilia to Film Studies', in Lee Grieveson and Haidee Wasson (eds), *Inventing Film Studies* (Durham, NC: Duke University Press, 2008), pp. 217–32 (p. 229).

10 Laura Mulvey, 'Cinema, Sync Sound and Europe 1929: Reflections on Coincidence', in Larry Sider, Diane Freeman and Jerry Sider (eds), *Soundscape: The School of Sound Lectures 1998–2001* (London: Wallflower Press, 2003), pp. 15–27 (p. 27).

11 Laura Mulvey, 'The Pleasure Principle', *Sight and Sound* 25, no. 6 (June 2015), pp. 50–1 (p. 51).

12 Ibid.

13 Conversation with Laura Mulvey, June 2023.

14 Ibid.

15 Laura Mulvey, 'Melodrama Inside and Outside the Home', in *Visual and Other Pleasures* (London: Palgrave, 2009 [1986]), pp. 66–81 (p. 77).

16 Scott MacDonald, *Screen Writings: Scripts and Texts by Independent Filmmakers* (Berkeley: University of California Press, 1995), p. 5.

17 Conversation with Laura Mulvey, 2016.

18 J. Hoberman, 'Our Mother, the Sphinx', *Village Voice*, XXIII, no. 10, 6 March 1978, p. 41.

19 Laura Mulvey, 'Visual Pleasure and Narrative Cinema', in *Visual and Other Pleasures* (London: Palgrave, 2009 [1975]), pp. 14–27 (p. 16).

20 Larry Sider, 'If You Wish to See, Listen: The Role of Sound Design', *Journal of Media Practice* 4, no. 1 (January 2003), pp. 5–15 (p. 7).

21 Ibid., p. 10.

22 So Mayer, 'Listening to Women', in Sue Clayton and Laura Mulvey (eds), *Other Cinemas: Politics, Culture and Experimental Film in the 1970s* (London: Bloomsbury, 2017), pp. 41–55 (p. 42).

23 Sigmund Freud, 'Remembering, Repeating and Working-Through (Further Recommendations on the Technique of Psycho-Analysis II)', in James Strachey (ed. and trans.),

The Standard Edition of the Complete Psychological Works of Sigmund Freud 12 (London: Hogarth Press, 1958 [1914]), pp. 145–56.

24 The script for 'Penthesilea: Queen of the Amazons' can be found in Oliver Fuke (ed.), *The Films of Laura Mulvey and Peter Wollen: Scripts, Working Documents, Interpretation* (London: BFI/Bloomsbury, 2023), pp. 37–60 (p. 40). This collection creates new possibilities for studying the written dimensions of their work.

25 Mary Ann Doane, *Femmes Fatales: Feminism, Film Theory, Psychoanalysis* (New York: Routledge, 1991), p. 170.

26 Laura Mulvey, 'Introduction', in Oliver Fuke (ed.), *The Films of Laura Mulvey and Peter Wollen: Scripts, Working Documents, Interpretation* (London: BFI/Bloomsbury, 2023), pp. 18–32 (p. 21).

27 Ibid., p. 22.

28 Peter Wollen, 'The Field of Language in Film', *October* 17 (Summer 1981), pp. 53–60 (p. 56).

29 The script for *Riddles of the Sphinx* can be found in Oliver Fuke (ed.), *The Films of Laura Mulvey and Peter Wollen: Scripts, Working Documents, Interpretation* (London: BFI/Bloomsbury, 2023), pp. 71–90 (p. 72).

30 Tony Rayns, 'Interview with Directors: Riddles of the Sphinx', *Time Out*, 6 May 1977, p. 15.

31 Nick Hart-Williams, 'Memories of The Other Cinema', in Sue Clayton and Laura Mulvey (eds), *Other Cinemas: Politics, Culture and Experimental Film in the 1970s* (London: Bloomsbury, 2017), pp. 273–8.

32 Mayer, 'Listening to Women', p. 44.

33 Roland Barthes, 'Garbo's Face', in *Mythologies: The Complete Edition*, trans. Richard Howard and Annette Lavers (New York: Hill & Wang, 2013 [1957]), pp. 73–5 (p. 73).

34 bell hooks 'The Oppositional Gaze: Black Female Spectators', in *Black Looks: Race and Representation* (Boston, MA: South End Press, 1992), pp. 115–31 (p. 119).

35 Laura Mulvey, 'Social Hieroglyphs: Reflections on Two Films by Douglas Sirk', in *Fetishism and Curiosity: Cinema and the Mind's Eye* (London: BFI/Palgrave, 2013 [1996]), pp. 34–51 (p. 45).

36 Peter Wollen, *Singin' in the Rain* (London: BFI/Palgrave, 2012 [1992]), pp. 67–8.

37 Ibid., p. 68.

38 Michel Chion, *The Voice in Cinema*, ed. and trans. Claudia Gorbman (New York: Columbia University Press, 1999 [1982]), pp. 17–29.

39 Kaja Silverman, *The Acoustic Mirror: The Female Voice in Psychoanalysis and Cinema* (Bloomington and Indianapolis: Indiana University Press, 1988), p. 130.

40 Nora M. Alter, *The Essay Film After Fact and Fiction* (New York: Columbia University Press, 2017), pp. 17–20.

41 Ibid., p. 4.

42 Laura Mulvey, 'Riddles as Essay Film', in Nora M. Alter and Timothy Corrigan (eds), *Essays on the Essay Film* (New York: Columbia University Press, 2017), pp. 314–21 (p. 314).

43 Alter, *The Essay Film After Fact and Fiction*, p. 13.

44 Ibid., p. 25.

45 Ibid., p. 26.

46 Alexandre Astruc, cited in Nora M. Alter, 'The Political Im/Perceptible in the Essay Film: Farocki's *Images of the World* *and the Inscription of War*', in Nora M. Alter and Timothy Corrigan (eds), *Essays on the Essay Film* (New York: Columbia University Press, 2017), pp. 134–60 (p. 138).

47 Wollen, 'The Field of Language in Film', p. 60.

48 Oliver Fuke, 'Introduction', in *The Films of Laura Mulvey and Peter Wollen: Scripts, Working Documents, Interpretation* (London: BFI/Bloomsbury, 2023), pp. 1–17 (p. 12).

49 Mulvey, 'Visual Pleasure and Narrative Cinema', p. 14.

50 Ibid., p. 15.

51 Wollen, 'Godard and Counter-Cinema', p. 79.

52 Peter Wollen, *Signs and Meaning in the Cinema* (London: BFI/Palgrave, 2013 [1969]).

53 Peter Wollen, 'The Two Avant-Gardes', in *Readings and Writings: Semiotic Counter-Strategies* (London: Verso, 1982 [1975]), pp. 92–104.

54 Ibid., p. 99.

55 Ibid., p. 100.

56 Graham Bennett, *Soft Machine: Out-Bloody-Rageous* (London: SAF Publishing, 2005).

57 Conversation with Laura Mulvey, April 2024.

58 Conversation with Larry Sider, January 2024.

59 Mayer, 'Listening to Women', p. 45.

60 Conversation with Laura Mulvey, June 2023.

61 Mulvey, 'Cinema, Sync Sound and Europe 1929', p. 15.

62 Silverman, *The Acoustic Mirror*, p. 100.

63 Laura Mulvey, 'Diane Tammes: Cinematographer', booklet accompanying the DVD of *Riddles of the Sphinx* (London: BFI, 2013), pp. 14–15 (p. 14).

64 Conversation with Laura Mulvey, June 2023.

65 Wollen, 'The Field of Language in Film', p. 53.

66 Julia Kristeva, 'The Semiotic *Chora* Ordering the Drives', in *Revolution in Poetic Language*, trans. Margaret Waller (New York: Columbia University Press, 1984), pp. 25–30 (pp. 26–7).

67 Ibid., pp. 25–30.

68 Laura Mulvey and Peter Wollen, 'Working Documents', in Oliver Fuke (ed.), *The Films of Laura Mulvey and Peter Wollen: Scripts, Working Documents, Interpretation* (London: BFI/Bloomsbury, 2023), pp. 341–57.

69 Julia Kristeva, 'Giotto's Joy', in Leon S. Roudiez (ed.), *Desire in Language: A Semiotic Approach to Literature and Art*, trans. Thomas Gora, Alice Jardine and Leon S. Roudiez (New York: Columbia University Press, 1980 [1972]), pp. 210–36 (p. 224).

70 Ibid., p. 225.

71 Juliet Mitchell, 'Women: The Longest Revolution', *New Left Review* 40 (November/December 1966), pp. 11–37 (p. 17).

72 Laura Mulvey, 'Chantal Akerman, *Jeanne Dielman, 23 Quai du commerce, 1080 Bruxelles*', in *Afterimages: On Cinema, Women and Changing Times* (London: Reaktion Books, 2019), pp. 99–112.

73 Kim Knowles, 'Engaging Material Specificities: Aesthetics and Politics in the 1970s', in Sue Clayton and Laura Mulvey (eds), *Other Cinemas: Politics,*

Culture and Experimental Film in the 1970s (London: Bloomsbury, 2017), pp. 107–20 (p. 108).

74 Mulvey, 'Diane Tammes: Cinematographer', p. 14.

75 Conversation with Laura Mulvey, April 2023.

76 Leslie Hills, 'Diane Tammes Obituary', *Guardian*, 20 June 2020. Available at: <https://www.theguardian.com/tv-and-radio/2020/jun/22/diane-tammes-obituary> (accessed August 2024).

77 Diane Tammes, 'Camerawoman Obscura: A "Personal" Account', *Women's Studies International Quarterly* 3, no. 1 (1980), pp. 59–61 (p. 60).

78 Association of Cinematograph and Television Technicians, *Patterns of Discrimination Against Women in the Film & Television Industries: A Special Report* (London: ACTT, 1975).

79 Laura Mulvey and Peter Wollen, 'Written Discussion', in Mark Webber (ed.), *The Afterimage Reader* (London: Visible Press, 2022 [1976]), pp. 165–73 (pp. 167–8).

80 Mulvey, *Afterimages*, p. 10.

81 Griselda Pollock, 'Modernity and the Spaces of Femininity', in *Vision and Difference: Femininity, Feminism and Histories of Art* (London and New York: Routledge, 1988), pp. 50–90.

82 Juliet Mitchell, *Woman's Estate* (New York: Pantheon Books, 1971), p. 62.

83 Sheila Rowbotham, *Woman's Consciousness, Man's World* (London and New York: Verso, 2015 [1973]), p. 29.

84 Ibid., pp. 29–30.

85 Sheila Rowbotham, Interview, in Michelene Wandor (ed.), *Once a Feminist: Stories of a Generation* (London: Virago Press, 1990), pp. 28–42 (p. 36).

86 Ibid.

87 Laura Mulvey, 'Introduction to the First Edition', in *Visual and Other Pleasures* (London: Palgrave, 2009 [1989]), pp. xxvii–xxxvi (p. xxviii).

88 Ibid.

89 Laura Mulvey and Margarita Jimenez, 'The Spectacle is Vulnerable: Miss World, 1970', in *Visual and Other Pleasures* (London: Palgrave, 2009 [1989]), pp. 3–5 (p. 3).

90 Helen Glew, '"Maiden, Whom We Never See": Cultural Representations of the "Lady Telephonist" in Britain ca. 1880–1930 and Institutional Responses', *Information & Culture* 55, no. 1 (February 2020), pp. 30–50.

91 Conversation with Laura Mulvey, April 2024.

92 Claire Johnston, 'Women's Cinema as Counter-Cinema', in Claire Johnston (ed.), *Notes on Women's Cinema* (London: Society for Education in Film and Television, 1973), pp. 24–31 (p. 31).

93 Rachel Pronger, '"It's All History if Only We Remember"', *Sight and Sound* 32, no. 7 (September 2022), pp. 9–10.

94 Sue Clayton and Laura Mulvey, 'Introduction', in Sue Clayton and Laura Mulvey (eds), *Other Cinemas: Politics, Culture and Experimental Film in the 1970s* (London: Bloomsbury, 2017), pp. 1–21 (p. 8).

95 Conversation with Larry Sider, January 2024.

96 Mulvey, 'Introduction', p. 21.

97 Stuart Hall and Paddy Whannel, *The Popular Arts* (Durham, NC: Duke University Press, 2018 [1964]).

98 Mulvey and Wollen, 'From Cinephilia to Film Studies', p. 217.

99 Sally Alexander, Interview, in Michelene Wandor (ed.), *Once a Feminist: Stories of a Generation* (London: Virago Press, 1990), pp. 81–92 (p. 91).

100 Conversation with Laura Mulvey, April 2023.

101 Mulvey, 'Chantal Akerman', p. 102.

102 Saidiya Hartman, 'The Belly of the World: A Note on Black Women's Labors', *Souls: A Critical Journal of Black Politics, Culture, and Society* 18, no. 1 (2016), pp. 166–73.

103 Isaac Julien and Kobena Mercer, 'Introduction: De Margin and De Centre', *Screen* 29, no. 4 (Autumn 1988), pp. 2–10 (p. 10).

104 Daniella Rose King, 'Britain's Black Filmmaking Workshops and Collective Practice', in Sue Clayton and Laura Mulvey (eds), *Other Cinemas: Politics, Culture and Experimental Film in the 1970s* (London: Bloomsbury, 2017), pp. 205–16.

105 Stuart Hall, 'Song of Handsworth Praise', *Guardian*, 15 January 1987, p. 12. Hall is defending the Black Audio Film Collective, which was aligned with Sankofa.

106 Isaac Julien, Commentary, 'Visual Pleasure at 40', *Screen* 56, no. 4 (Winter 2015), pp. 475–7 (p. 476).

107 Ibid., p. 477.

108 Wollen, 'The Field of Language in Film', p. 56.

109 Mayer, 'Listening to Women', p. 49.

110 hooks, 'The Oppositional Gaze', p. 118.

111 Ibid., p. 125.

112 Ibid., p. 124.

113 Conversation with Laura Mulvey, April 2024.

114 Ibid.

115 Mulvey, 'Melodrama Inside and Outside the Home', p. 78.

116 Ibid., pp. 73, 79.

117 Mulvey, 'Social Hieroglyphs: Reflections on Two Films by Douglas Sirk', pp. 34–51.

118 Laura Mulvey, Commentary, BFI DVD *Riddles of the Sphinx* (London: BFI, 2013).

119 Email conversation with Larry Sider, March 2024.

120 Wollen, 'The Field of Language in Film', p. 56.

121 Jacqueline Rose, *Women in Dark Times* (London: Bloomsbury, 2014), p. ix.

122 Mulvey, 'Introduction to the First Edition', p. xxxii.

123 Mulvey, 'Introduction', p. 27.

Credits

Riddles of the Sphinx
UK
1977

Written and Directed by
Laura Mulvey
Peter Wollen
Production
BFI Production Board
Rostrum
Frameline Productions
Lights
G.B.S.
Opticals
Herbert Maiden
Video
Evanston Percussion Unit
Production Assistance
Mark Nash
Linda Redford
John Howe
Jonathan Collinson
Childcare
Christine Smith
Sound
Larry Sider
Editing
Carola Klein
Larry Sider
Sound Mix
Peter Maxwell
Cinematography
Diane Tammes
Assisted by
Jane Jackson
Steve Shaw
Music
Mike Ratledge

**Performed with
Equipment Designed by**
Denys Irving

© British Film Institute
1977

CAST
Dinah Stabb
Louise
Merdelle Jordine
Maxine
Rhiannon Tise
Anna
Clive Merrison
Chris
Marie Green
acrobat
Paula Melbourne
rope act
Crissie Trigger
juggler
Mary Maddox
voice off
Laura Mulvey
Mary Kelly
Marion Dain
Rosalind Delmar
Mary Dickinson
Rosamund Howe
Miranda Feuchtwang
Carole James
Claire Johnston
Tina Keane
Lin Layram
Carole Myer
Patsy Nightingale
Brenda Prince
Valerie Neale

Winifred Wollen
Joy Wong
**Staff of the Kensington
Training School**

**Locations by
Courtesy of**
Arndale Centre
Elona Bennett and Paul
Butler
British Museum
Steve Dwoskin
Holloway Neighbourhood
Group
Inner London Education
Authority
Judith and Malcom Le
Grice
Oval House
Post Office
Chad Wollen

**Grateful
Acknowledgments to**
Berwick Street Film
Collective
Rosalind Delmar
Mary Kelly
Carol Laws
Midi-Minuit Fantastique
Griselda Pollock

Film material by
permission of the
Egyptian Tourist Office,
Movietone, Mark Peploe,
C. H. Wood (Bradford) Ltd

Production Details
16mm
1.33:1
Colour
Running time:
91 minutes

Bibliography

Alexander, Sally, Interview, in Michelene Wandor (ed.), *Once a Feminist: Stories of a Generation* (London: Virago Press, 1990), pp. 81–92.

Alter, Nora M., *The Essay Film After Fact and Fiction* (New York: Columbia University Press, 2017).

Alter, Nora M., 'The Political Im/ Perceptible in the Essay Film: Farocki's *Images of the World and the Inscription of War*', in Nora M. Alter and Timothy Corrigan (eds), *Essays on the Essay Film* (New York: Columbia University Press, 2017), pp. 134–60.

Association of Cinematograph and Television Technicians, *Patterns of Discrimination Against Women in the Film & Television Industries: A Special Report* (London: ACTT, 1975).

Barthes, Roland, 'Garbo's Face', in *Mythologies: The Complete Edition*, trans. Richard Howard and Annette Lavers (New York: Hill & Wang, 2013 [1957]), pp. 73–5.

Bennett, Graham, *Soft Machine: Out-Bloody-Rageous* (London: SAF Publishing, 2005).

Chion, Michel, *The Voice in Cinema*, trans. and ed. Claudia Gorbman (New York: Columbia University Press, 1999 [1982]).

Clayton, Sue and Laura Mulvey, 'Introduction', in Sue Clayton and Laura Mulvey (eds), *Other Cinemas: Politics, Culture and Experimental Film in the 1970s* (London: Bloomsbury, 2017), pp. 1–21.

Doane, Mary Ann, *Femmes Fatales: Feminism, Film Theory, Psychoanalysis* (New York: Routledge, 1991).

Freud, Sigmund, 'Remembering, Repeating and Working-Through (Further Recommendations on the Technique of Psycho-Analysis II)', in James Strachey (ed. and trans.), *The Standard Edition of the Complete Psychological Works of Sigmund Freud* 12 (London: Hogarth Press, 1958 [1914]), pp. 145–56.

Fuke, Oliver, 'Introduction', in Oliver Fuke (ed.), *The Films of Laura Mulvey and Peter Wollen: Scripts, Working Documents, Interpretation* (London: BFI/Bloomsbury, 2023), pp. 1–17.

Glew, Helen, '"Maiden, Whom We Never See": Cultural Representations of the "Lady Telephonist" in Britain ca. 1880–1930 and Institutional Responses', *Information & Culture* 55, no. 1 (February 2020), pp. 30–50.

Hall, Stuart, 'Song of Handsworth Praise', *Guardian*, 15 January 1987, p. 12.

Hall, Stuart and Paddy Whannel, *The Popular Arts* (Durham, NC: Duke University Press, 2018 [1964]).

Hammond, Simon, 'Knight's Moves', *New Left Review* 124 (July/August 2020), pp. 5–40.

Hart-Williams, Nick, 'Memories of The Other Cinema', in Sue Clayton and Laura Mulvey (eds), *Other Cinemas: Politics, Culture and Experimental Film in the 1970s* (London: Bloomsbury, 2017), pp. 273–8.

Hartman, Saidiya, 'The Belly of the World: A Note on Black Women's Labors', *Souls: A Critical Journal of Black Politics, Culture, and Society* 18, no. 1 (2016), pp. 166–73.

Hills, Leslie, 'Diane Tammes Obituary', *Guardian*, 20 June 2020. Available at: <https://www.theguardian.com/tv-and-radio/2020/jun/22/diane-tammes-obituary> (accessed August 2024).

Hoberman, J., 'Our Mother, the Sphinx', *Village Voice*, XXIII, no. 10, 6 March 1978, p. 41.

hooks, bell, 'The Oppositional Gaze: Black Female Spectators', in *Black Looks: Race and Representation* (Boston, MA: South End Press, 1992), pp. 115–31.

Johnston, Claire, 'Women's Cinema as Counter-Cinema', in Claire Johnston (ed.), *Notes on Women's Cinema* (London: Society for Education in Film and Television, 1973), pp. 24–31.

Julien, Isaac, Commentary, 'Visual Pleasure at 40', *Screen* 56, no. 4 (Winter 2015), pp. 475–7.

Julien, Isaac and Kobena Mercer, 'Introduction: De Margin and De Centre', *Screen* 29, no. 4 (Autumn 1988), pp. 2–10.

King, Daniella Rose, 'Britain's Black Filmmaking Workshops and Collective Practice', in Sue Clayton and Laura Mulvey (eds), *Other Cinemas: Politics, Culture and Experimental Film in the 1970s* (London: Bloomsbury, 2017), pp. 205–16.

Knowles, Kim, 'Engaging Material Specificities: Aesthetics and Politics in the 1970s', in Sue Clayton and Laura Mulvey (eds), *Other Cinemas: Politics, Culture and Experimental Film in the 1970s* (London: Bloomsbury, 2017), pp. 107–20.

Kristeva, Julia, 'Giotto's Joy', in Leon S. Roudiez (ed.), *Desire in Language: A Semiotic Approach to Literature and Art*, trans. Thomas Gora, Alice Jardine and Leon S. Roudiez (New York: Columbia University Press, 1980 [1972]), pp. 210–36.

Kristeva, Julia, 'The Semiotic *Chora* Ordering the Drives', in *Revolution in Poetic Language*, trans. Margaret Waller (New York: Columbia University Press, 1984), pp. 25–30.

MacDonald, Scott, *Screen Writings: Scripts and Texts by Independent Filmmakers* (Berkeley: University of California Press, 1995).

Mayer, So, 'Listening to Women', in Sue Clayton and Laura Mulvey (eds), *Other Cinemas: Politics, Culture and Experimental Film in the 1970s* (London: Bloomsbury, 2017), pp. 41–55.

Mitchell, Juliet, 'Women: The Longest Revolution', *New Left Review* 40 (November/December 1966), pp. 11–37.

Mitchell, Juliet, *Woman's Estate* (New York: Pantheon Books, 1971).

Mulvey, Laura, 'Cinema, Sync Sound and Europe 1929: Reflections on Coincidence', in Larry Sider, Diane Freeman and Jerry Sider (eds), *Soundscape: The School of Sound Lectures 1998–2001* (London: Wallflower Press, 2003), pp. 15–27.

Mulvey, Laura, 'Introduction to the First Edition', in *Visual and Other Pleasures* (London: Palgrave, 2009 [1989]), pp. xxvii–xxxvi.

Mulvey, Laura, 'Melodrama Inside and Outside the Home', in *Visual and*

Other Pleasures (London: Palgrave, 2009 [1986]), pp. 66–81.

Mulvey, Laura, 'Visual Pleasure and Narrative Cinema', in *Visual and Other Pleasures* (London: Palgrave, 2009 [1975]), pp. 14–27.

Mulvey, Laura, 'Americanitis: European Intellectuals and Hollywood Melodrama', in *Fetishism and Curiosity: Cinema and the Mind's Eye* (London: BFI/Palgrave, 2013 [1996]), pp. 19–33.

Mulvey, Laura, 'Diane Tammes: Cinematographer', booklet accompanying the DVD of *Riddles of the Sphinx* (London: BFI, 2013), pp. 14–15.

Mulvey, Laura, 'Social Hieroglyphs: Reflections on Two Films by Douglas Sirk', in *Fetishism and Curiosity: Cinema and the Mind's Eye* (London: BFI/Palgrave, 2013 [1996]), pp. 34–51.

Mulvey, Laura, 'The Pleasure Principle', *Sight and Sound* 25, no. 6 (June 2015), pp. 50–1.

Mulvey, Laura, 'Riddles as Essay Film', in Nora M. Alter and Timothy Corrigan (eds), *Essays on the Essay Film* (New York: Columbia University Press, 2017), pp. 314–21.

Mulvey, Laura, *Afterimages: On Cinema, Women and Changing Times* (London: Reaktion Books, 2019).

Mulvey, Laura, 'Chantal Akerman, *Jeanne Dielman, 23 Quai du commerce, 1080 Bruxelles*', in *Afterimages: On Cinema, Women and Changing Times* (London: Reaktion Books, 2019), pp. 99–112.

Mulvey, Laura, 'Introduction', in Oliver Fuke (ed.), *The Films of Laura Mulvey and Peter Wollen: Scripts, Working Documents, Interpretation* (London: BFI/Bloomsbury, 2023), pp. 18–33.

Mulvey, Laura and Margarita Jimenez, 'The Spectacle is Vulnerable: Miss World, 1970', in *Visual and Other Pleasures* (London: Palgrave, 2009 [1989]), pp. 3–5.

Mulvey, Laura and Peter Wollen, 'From Cinephilia to Film Studies', in Lee Grieveson and Haidee Wasson (eds), *Inventing Film Studies* (Durham, NC: Duke University Press, 2008), pp. 217–32.

Mulvey, Laura and Peter Wollen, 'Written Discussion', in Mark Webber (ed.), *The Afterimage Reader* (London: Visible Press, 2022 [1976]), pp. 165–73.

Mulvey, Laura and Peter Wollen, 'Penthesilea: Queen of the Amazons', Script, in Oliver Fuke (ed.), *The Films of Laura Mulvey and Peter Wollen: Scripts, Working Documents, Interpretation* (London: BFI/Bloomsbury, 2023), pp. 37–60.

Mulvey, Laura and Peter Wollen, 'Riddles of the Sphinx', Script, in Oliver Fuke (ed.), *The Films of Laura Mulvey and Peter Wollen: Scripts, Working Documents, Interpretation* (London: BFI/Bloomsbury, 2023), pp. 71–98.

Mulvey, Laura and Peter Wollen, 'Working Documents', in Oliver Fuke (ed.), *The Films of Laura Mulvey and Peter Wollen: Scripts, Working Documents, Interpretation* (London: BFI/Bloomsbury, 2023), pp. 341–57.

Pollock, Griselda, 'Modernity and the Spaces of Femininity', in *Vision and*

Difference: Femininity, Feminism and Histories of Art (London and New York: Routledge, 1988), pp. 50–90.

Pollock, Griselda and Laura Mulvey, 'Laura Mulvey in Conversation with Griselda Pollock', *Studies in the Maternal* 2, no. 1 (2010), pp. 1–13. Available at: <https://doi.org/10.16995/sim.101> (accessed August 2024).

Pronger, Rachel, '"It's All History if Only We Remember"', *Sight and Sound* 32, no. 7 (September 2022), pp. 9–10.

Rayns, Tony, 'Interview with Directors: Riddles of the Sphinx', *Time Out*, 6 May 1977, p. 15.

Rose, Jacqueline, *Women in Dark Times* (London: Bloomsbury, 2014).

Rowbotham, Sheila, Interview, in Michelene Wandor (ed.), *Once a Feminist: Stories of a Generation* (London: Virago Press, 1990), pp. 28–42.

Rowbotham, Sheila, *Woman's Consciousness, Man's World* (London and New York: Verso, 2015 [1973]).

Sider, Larry, 'If You Wish to See, Listen: The Role of Sound Design', *Journal of Media Practice* 4, no. 1 (January 2003), pp. 5–15.

Silverman, Kaja, *The Acoustic Mirror: The Female Voice in Psychoanalysis and Cinema* (Bloomington and Indianapolis: Indiana University Press, 1988).

Tammes, Diane, 'Camerawoman Obscura: A "Personal" Account', *Women's Studies International Quarterly* 3, no. 1 (1980), pp. 59–61.

Wollen, Peter, 'The Field of Language in Film', *October* 17 (Summer 1981), pp. 53–60.

Wollen, Peter, 'Godard and Counter-Cinema: Vent d'Est', in *Readings and Writings: Semiotic Counter-Strategies* (London: Verso, 1982 [1972]), pp. 79–91.

Wollen, Peter, 'The Two Avant-Gardes', in *Readings and Writings: Semiotic Counter-Strategies* (London: Verso, 1982 [1975]), pp. 92–104.

Wollen, Peter, 'An Alphabet of Cinema', in *Paris Hollywood: Writings on Film* (London and New York: Verso Books, 2002 [2001]), pp. 1–21.

Wollen, Peter, *Singin' in the Rain* (London: BFI/Palgrave, 2012 [1992]).

Wollen, Peter, *Signs and Meaning in the Cinema* (London: BFI/Palgrave, 2013 [1969]).